Microsoft® Office Word 2016: Part 2

Microsoft® Office Word 2016: Part 2

Part Number: 091049
Course Edition: 1.1

Acknowledgements

PROJECT TEAM

Author	Media Designer	Content Editor
Rozanne Murphy Whalen	Brian Sullivan	Joe McElveney

Logical Operations wishes to thank the Logical Operations Instructor Community, and in particular Ketta Nanna and Mickey Curry, for contributing their technical and instructional expertise during the creation of this course.

Notices

DISCLAIMER

While Logical Operations, Inc. takes care to ensure the accuracy and quality of these materials, we cannot guarantee their accuracy, and all materials are provided without any warranty whatsoever, including, but not limited to, the implied warranties of merchantability or fitness for a particular purpose. The name used in the data files for this course is that of a fictitious company. Any resemblance to current or future companies is purely coincidental. We do not believe we have used anyone's name in creating this course, but if we have, please notify us and we will change the name in the next revision of the course. Logical Operations is an independent provider of integrated training solutions for individuals, businesses, educational institutions, and government agencies. The use of screenshots, photographs of another entity's products, or another entity's product name or service in this book is for editorial purposes only. No such use should be construed to imply sponsorship or endorsement of the book by nor any affiliation of such entity with Logical Operations. This courseware may contain links to sites on the Internet that are owned and operated by third parties (the "External Sites"). Logical Operations is not responsible for the availability of, or the content located on or through, any External Site. Please contact Logical Operations if you have any concerns regarding such links or External Sites.

TRADEMARK NOTICES

Microsoft® Office Word 2016: Part 2

About This Course

After you master the basics of using Microsoft® Word 2016 such as creating, editing, and saving documents; navigating through a document; and printing, you're ready to move on to tackling the more advanced features. These features enable you to create complex and professional documents with a consistent look and feel. They also enable you to automate tedious tasks such as preparing a letter to send to every customer of your organization.

Creating professional-looking documents can help you give your organization a competitive edge. Implementing time-saving features such as document templates and automated mailings helps your organization reduce expenses. Mastering these techniques will make you a valued employee in your organization.

This course covers Microsoft Office Specialist exam objectives to help students prepare for the Word 2016 Exam and the Word 2016 Expert Exam.

Course Description

Target Student

This course is designed for students who wish to use Microsoft Word to create and modify complex documents and use tools that allow them to customize those documents.

Course Prerequisites

To ensure your success in this course, you should have end-user skills with any current version of Windows®, including being able to start programs, switch between programs, locate saved files, close programs, and access websites using a web browser. In addition, you should be able to navigate and perform common tasks in Word, such as opening, viewing, editing, and saving documents; formatting text and paragraphs; format the overall appearance of a page; and create lists and tables. To meet these prerequisites, you can take any one or more of the following Logical Operations courses:

- *Microsoft® Office Word 2016: Part 1*
- *Using Microsoft® Windows® 10* or *Microsoft® Windows® 10: Transition from Windows® 7*

Course Objectives

In this course, you will learn to create and modify complex documents and use tools that allow you to customize those documents.

You will:

- Organize content using tables and charts.
- Customize formats using styles and themes.
- Insert content using quick parts.
- Use templates to automate document formatting.

- Control the flow of a document.
- Simplify and manage long documents.
- Use mail merge to create letters, envelopes, and labels.

The CHOICE Home Screen

Logon and access information for your CHOICE environment will be provided with your class experience. The CHOICE platform is your entry point to the CHOICE learning experience, of which this course manual is only one part.

On the CHOICE Home screen, you can access the CHOICE Course screens for your specific courses. Visit the CHOICE Course screen both during and after class to make use of the world of support and instructional resources that make up the CHOICE experience.

Each CHOICE Course screen will give you access to the following resources:

- **Classroom**: A link to your training provider's classroom environment.
- **eBook**: An interactive electronic version of the printed book for your course.
- **Files**: Any course files available to download.
- **Checklists**: Step-by-step procedures and general guidelines you can use as a reference during and after class.
- **LearnTOs**: Brief animated videos that enhance and extend the classroom learning experience.
- **Assessment**: A course assessment for your self-assessment of the course content.
- Social media resources that enable you to collaborate with others in the learning community using professional communications sites such as LinkedIn or microblogging tools such as Twitter.

Depending on the nature of your course and the components chosen by your learning provider, the CHOICE Course screen may also include access to elements such as:

- LogicalLABS, a virtual technical environment for your course.
- Various partner resources related to the courseware.
- Related certifications or credentials.
- A link to your training provider's website.
- Notices from the CHOICE administrator.
- Newsletters and other communications from your learning provider.
- Mentoring services.

Visit your CHOICE Home screen often to connect, communicate, and extend your learning experience!

How to Use This Book

As You Learn

This book is divided into lessons and topics, covering a subject or a set of related subjects. In most cases, lessons are arranged in order of increasing proficiency.

The results-oriented topics include relevant and supporting information you need to master the content. Each topic has various types of activities designed to enable you to solidify your understanding of the informational material presented in the course. Information is provided for reference and reflection to facilitate understanding and practice.

Data files for various activities as well as other supporting files for the course are available by download from the CHOICE Course screen. In addition to sample data for the course exercises, the course files may contain media components to enhance your learning and additional reference materials for use both during and after the course.

Checklists of procedures and guidelines can be used during class and as after-class references when you're back on the job and need to refresh your understanding.

At the back of the book, you will find a glossary of the definitions of the terms and concepts used throughout the course. You will also find an index to assist in locating information within the instructional components of the book.

As You Review

Any method of instruction is only as effective as the time and effort you, the student, are willing to invest in it. In addition, some of the information that you learn in class may not be important to you immediately, but it may become important later. For this reason, we encourage you to spend some time reviewing the content of the course after your time in the classroom.

As a Reference

The organization and layout of this book make it an easy-to-use resource for future reference. Taking advantage of the glossary, index, and table of contents, you can use this book as a first source of definitions, background information, and summaries.

Course Icons

Watch throughout the material for the following visual cues.

Icon	Description
	A **Note** provides additional information, guidance, or hints about a topic or task.
	A **Caution** note makes you aware of places where you need to be particularly careful with your actions, settings, or decisions so that you can be sure to get the desired results of an activity or task.
	LearnTO notes show you where an associated LearnTO is particularly relevant to the content. Access LearnTOs from your CHOICE Course screen.
	Checklists provide job aids you can use after class as a reference to perform skills back on the job. Access checklists from your CHOICE Course screen.
	Social notes remind you to check your CHOICE Course screen for opportunities to interact with the CHOICE community using social media.

1 Organizing Content Using Tables and Charts

Lesson Time: 45 minutes

Lesson Objectives

In this lesson, you will organize content using tables and charts. You will:

- Sort the rows in a table.

- Manage the display of a cell.

- Calculate values using mathematical formulas.

- Create a chart.

- Embed and link an Excel table in a Word document.

Lesson Introduction

You use tables in documents so that you can arrange information in rows and columns. But you can use tables for more than just making your data look good. In this lesson, you will organize and chart the data in tables.

TOPIC A

Sort Table Data

When you enter data into a table, you probably are not entering it in any specific order; just the order you receive the information. You could cut and paste the information to put it in alphabetical or numerical order, but this is time consuming and you could still end up not having everything in perfect order. Microsoft® Word enables you to easily sort the table data into meaningful groups.

Table Sorting

Sorting data in a table puts the data in ascending or descending alphabetical or numerical order. You can sort tables on a single level or on multiple levels. For example, if you are sorting a list of customers, you might first sort by city, then by ZIP code if there are numerous ZIP codes within the city, and then by street.

It is not necessary to have column headings, but it makes it easier and more meaningful if the columns do have headings. You can refer to the headings when sorting in Word. If you have headings but don't indicate that you do in the **Sort** dialog box by selecting the **Header row** option, Word sorts the column headings with the rest of the data and thus the headings won't remain at the top of the columns.

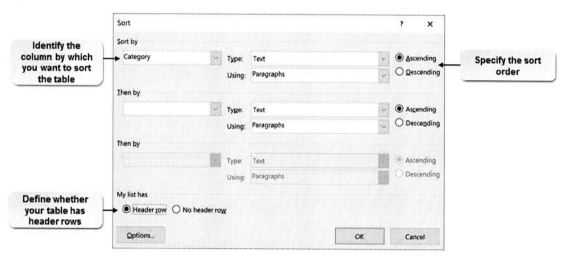

Figure 1–1: Sort dialog box configured for a single–level sort.

> **Note:** Tables containing merged cells cannot be sorted.

Word 2016 supports multiple levels of sorting. For example, you can perform the type of sort that you see in phone books: Phone books are sorted in order first by last name, and then within the same last name, in order by first name. To perform a multiple-level sort, you add the column(s) by which you want to sort using the **Then by** drop-down lists.

> Access the Checklist tile on your CHOICE Course screen for reference information and job aids on **How to Sort Table Data**.

ACTIVITY 1–1
Sorting Table Data

Data File

Desktop\Building with Heart\Organizing Content Using Tables and Charts\Inventory.docx

Scenario

Building with Heart is a non-profit volunteer organization that helps families in need buy affordable, safe, and healthy homes. As a Building with Heart staff member, you have been asked to organize the inventory list for HouSalvage. HouSalvage is Building with Heart's retail store that offers recycled construction materials at a reduced price. HouSalvage has received a number of items that another staffer has added to the Inventory file. The staffer added items to the inventory table in no particular order. You want to sort the inventory in order by category and then by item name.

 Note: Activities may vary slightly if the software vendor has issued digital updates. Your instructor will notify you of any changes.

1. Open the inventory from the Windows Desktop.

   a) On your Windows Desktop, open the **Building with Heart** folder. Then open the **Organizing Content Using Tables and Charts** folder.

   b) Open **Inventory.docx**.

   Microsoft Word opens and displays the contents of the Inventory file.

2. Perform a single-level sort of the inventory table by category.

   a) Scroll through the document and notice that most of the rows of the table are not in order by category.

   b) Click within the five-column table to enable the **Table Tools** contextual tabs.

   c) Select the **Table Tools Layout** tab.

   d) In the **Data** group, select **Sort**. Notice that Word selects the entire table automatically.

e) Under **My list has**, select **Header row** to specify that you want to exclude the first row of the table from the sort.

My list has

◉ Header row   ○ No header row

f) Under **Sort by**, in the first drop-down list, verify that **Category** is selected.

g) Under **Then by**, verify that the first drop-down list is empty. Even though the **Type** and **Using** drop-down lists are pre-filled in, Word performs only a single-level sort because the **Then by** drop-down list is empty.

Sort	? ✕
Sort by	
Category ▾ Type: Text ▾	◉ Ascending
Using: Paragraphs ▾	○ Descending
Then by	
▾ Type: Text ▾	◉ Ascending
Using: Paragraphs ▾	○ Descending
Then by	
▾ Type: Text ▾	◉ Ascending
Using: Paragraphs ▾	○ Descending
My list has	
◉ Header row ○ No header row	
Options...	OK Cancel

h) Select **OK**.

i) Scroll through the table to verify that all of the rows in the inventory table are now sorted by category. Notice that within the category, Word didn't sort the items by item name.

3. Perform a two-level sort of the table by category and then by item name.

a) On the **Table Tools Layout** tab, select **Sort**. Under **My list has**, select **Header row**.

b) Under **Then by**, in the drop-down list, select **Item Name**.

Sort		? X
Sort by		
Category ∨	Type: Text ∨	● Ascending
	Using: Paragraphs ∨	○ Descending
Then by		
Item Name ∨	Type: Text ∨	● Ascending
	Using: Paragraphs ∨	○ Descending
Then by		
∨	Type: Text ∨	● Ascending
	Using: Paragraphs ∨	○ Descending
My list has		
● Header row ○ No header row		
Options...		OK Cancel

c) Select **OK**.

d) Scroll through the table to verify that the list is sorted by category, and that within each category, Word sorted the inventory by item name.

Category	Item Name	Wholesale Price	Retail Price	Quantity on Hand
Appliances	Dishwasher	$99.95		4
Appliances	Electric cooktop	$125.99		2
Appliances	Electric front-loading washer	$119.99		6
Appliances	Electric top-loading washer	$69.99		3
Appliances	Electric water heater (50	$139.99		2

 Note: To simplify saving documents with new names throughout the class, you are going to add the **Save as** command to the **Quick Access Toolbar**.

4. Customize the **Quick Access Toolbar** to include the **Save As** command.

a) Select the **drop-down arrow** on the **Quick Access Toolbar** and then select **More Commands**.

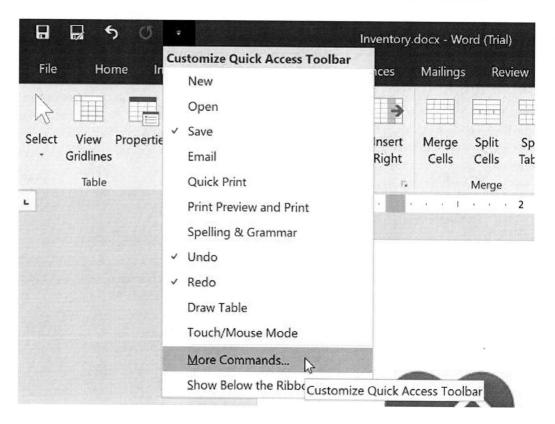

b) Below **Choose commands from**, select **Save As**.

c) Select **Add**.

d) Below **Customize Quick Access Toolbar**, select the **Save As** command and select the **Move Up** button until **Save As** is directly below **Save**.

e) Select **OK** to save your changes. You now see the **Save As** command immediately after the **Save** command on the **Quick Access Toolbar**.

5. Save the file in the **Organizing Content Using Tables and Charts** folder as *My Inventory*

   a) On the **Quick Access Toolbar**, click **Save As**.

   b) Verify that the current folder is **Desktop\Building with Heart\Organizing Content Using Tables and Charts**.

   c) In the **File name** text box, type *My Inventory*

   d) Select **Save**.

Note: For more information, check out LearnTO **Simplify the Opening and Saving of Word Documents** from the **LearnTO** tile on your CHOICE Course screen.

TOPIC B

Control Cell Layout

You have sorted the data in a table. Some of the data in a column might apply to multiple rows of data. You could leave the redundant information in each row, or you could combine those redundant cells into a single cell to make the data more readable. By controlling the cell layout, you can change the shape and arrangement of the cells within the table and change the direction the text flows within cells.

Cell Merging

Cell merging combines multiple adjacent cells into a single cell that is the size and shape of the original cells. You can combine cells from rows, columns, or both.

Cells merged from two columns and three rows to create this cell			Cells merged from five rows to create this cell		
Cells merged from five columns to create this cell					

Figure 1–2: Merged table cells.

Merging cells is useful when you want to add a title that goes across all the rows in a table or when you have sorted data and want the common information listed just once for the grouping where it applies.

 Building with **Heart**

HouSalvage Greene City Inventory				
Category	Item Name	Retail Price	Quantity on Hand	Value
Appliances	Dishwasher	$99.95	4	
	Electric cooktop	$125.99	2	
	Electric front-loading washer	$119.99	6	
	Electric top-loading washer	$69.99	3	
	Electric water heater (50 gallons)	$139.99	2	
	Gas cooktop	$149.99	7	
	Gas water heater (50 gallons)	$159.99	7	
	Refrigerator side by side—25.4 cubic feet	$499.99	3	
Cabinets	Maple kitchen	$229.99	8	
	Oak kitchen	$109.99	11	

Figure 1-3: Merged title row and category cells.

If data already exists in the cells before you merge them, Word will list the data in the merged cell as multiple paragraphs. In the example in the previous figure, "Appliances" was listed on each row of the table for the items adjacent to the merged **Appliances** cell. When Word initially merged the cells, it listed "Appliances" eight times within the merged cell. The person who merged the cells then deleted all except one instance of the word.

 Caution: If your table contains merged cells, you cannot sort the entire table. You can select only a portion of the table that contains unmerged cells and perform a sort on the selected cells.

Cell Splitting

Cell splitting divides one or more cells into multiple adjacent cells. If you are splitting a single cell into two or more cells, you can right-click the cell and select **Split Cell**. If you are splitting multiple cells, you can do so only from the **Table Tools Layout** tab.

Cell Alignment

The *cell alignment* options on the **Table Tools Layout** tab, in the **Alignment** group, enable you to position the cell contents in one of nine positions. The buttons show the alignment positioning. The alignment choices are top left, top center, top right, center left, center center, center right, bottom left, bottom center, and bottom right.

Text Direction

Text direction options in the **Alignment** group of the **Table Tools Layout** tab enable you to position the text horizontally or vertically in a table cell. The default is horizontal. You can turn it 90 degrees and flow up the left side of the cell or down the right side of the cell.

 Access the Checklist tile on your CHOICE Course screen for reference information and job aids on How to Control Cell Layout.

ACTIVITY 1-2
Controlling Cell Layout

Before You Begin

My Inventory.docx is open.

Scenario

Your manager asked you to make the inventory listing for the Greene City chapter of HouSalvage easier to view, especially differentiating where each category of item begins in the table. The table currently has no title, and you think a title across the top of the table would help identify the purpose of the table. You want to eliminate redundant category names since all of the data is sorted into categories. To make the table more attractive, you want to change the text direction so that it fits within the merged cells. Your finished document will look like the following example.

HouSalvage Greene City Inventory				
Category	Item Name	Wholesale Price	Retail Price	Quantity on Hand
Appliances	Dishwasher	$99.95		4
	Electric cooktop	$125.99		2
	Electric front-loading washer	$119.99		6
	Electric top-loading washer	$69.99		3
	Electric water heater (50 gallons)	$139.99		2
	Gas cooktop	$149.99		7
	Gas water heater (50 gallons)	$159.99		7
	Refrigerator side by side—25.4 cubic feet	$499.99		3

1. Merge cells in a new row added to the top of the table for a title.
   a) Select the first row of the table.

   > **Note:** Remember, to select a row in a table, you can either drag over the cells and select them or click to the left just outside the table to select the row.

   b) On the **Table Tools Layout** tab, in the **Rows & Columns** group, select **Insert Above**.
   c) With the new row selected, in the **Merge** group, select **Merge Cells**.
   d) Type *HouSalvage Greene City Inventory*

2. Center align the title text.
   a) Verify that your cursor is still in the title row of the table.

b) On the **Table Tools Layout** tab, in the **Alignment** group, select the **Align Center** button to center the title in the cell.

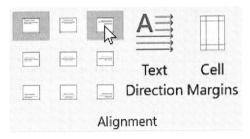

3. Right align the **Quantity on Hand** column.
   a) In the **Quantity on Hand** column, select all the numbers.
   b) In the **Alignment** group, select the **Align Top Right** button to right align the numbers.

4. Merge each grouping of categories into a single cell and then change the text direction to flow up the left side of the cell.
   a) Select all of the **Appliances** cells in the first column.

 Note: One easy way to select all the cells in the column is to select the first cell, scroll down to where you can see the last cell, then hold down **Shift** and select the last cell. Word selects all the cells in the column.

   b) On the **Table Tools Layout** tab, in the **Alignment** group, select **Merge Cells**.

 Note: Alternatively, you can right-click and select **Merge Cells**.

   c) Delete all of the words, leaving just one instance of "Appliances."
   d) On the **Table Tools Layout** tab, in the **Merge** group, select the **Text Direction** button twice. The first time you select it, the text flows down the right side of the cell; the second time, it flows up the left side of the cell.

e) Select **Align Center Left**.

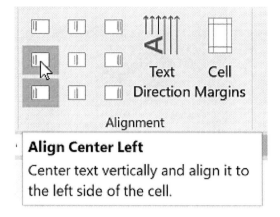

f) Save the file.

TOPIC C

Perform Calculations in a Table

You have sorted table data and arranged the table layout. You can also manage table data through simple calculations on data in the table.

Word is most appropriate for creating text documents, but it can also perform simple calculations. Word enables you to insert formulas and functions into your document so that you can perform calculations on numbers in the document.

Formulas in Word

A *formula* is a type of field code you use to perform mathematical calculations on data in a table. You can perform mathematical operations such as adding, subtracting, or averaging the numbers in a row or column. You can also enter numbers directly into the formula. By default, the formula adds the numbers above or to the left of the cell in which you insert the formula.

You must always begin a formula with an equal sign, then add one of the following:

- A function (for example, SUM or AVERAGE) and arguments (ABOVE, BELOW, LEFT, specific cells, numbers, bookmarks, and more).
- Numbers and operators (for example, =32*.25).
- A combination of the two.

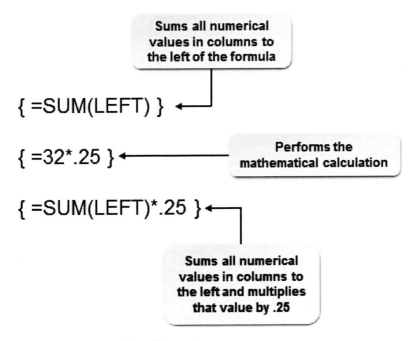

Figure 1-4: Examples of formulas.

Formulas are stored in Word as field codes. If you want to see the field codes, press **Alt+F9**. Press **Alt+F9** again to toggle back to the results. If you are working on a tablet, perform a right-click action on the formula's results and select **Toggle Field Codes**.

The **Formula** option is available on the **Table Tools Layout** tab in the **Data** group. Word displays this contextual tab only when your cursor is somewhere within the table.

Updating Results

Word doesn't automatically update the formula results when you change a number. Word updates the formula results when you open the document, or you can manually update the results. To manually update the calculation, select the field and then press **F9**, or right-click the field and then select **Update field**. To update all calculations in the table or document, select the entire table or document before you press **F9**.

You can also prevent Word from updating a formula. To lock a formula to prevent updates, select the formula and then press **Ctrl+F11**. To unlock the formula, select it and then press **Ctrl+Shift +F11**.

Number Format

An optional feature in the **Formula** dialog box is to format the number that Word calculates with your formula. There are several masks in the **Number format** list. The *mask* specifies the format in which Word displays the numbers, such as formatting with dollar signs or percent signs and the number of decimal places to use. The following table describes the available number format masks and contains examples of each mask.

Number Format Mask	Description
#,##0	Displays whole numbers with commas to separate thousands, millions, and so on.
#,##0.00	Displays numbers with two decimal places and commas to separate thousands, millions, and so on.
$#,##0.00; ($#,##0.00)	Displays numbers preceded by the dollar sign ($), followed by two decimal places, and with commas to separate thousands, millions, and so on. In addition, displays negative numbers in parentheses.
0	Displays whole numbers only without commas to separate thousands, millions, and so on.
0%	Displays decimal values as percentages.
0.00	Displays numbers with two decimal places and no comma separators.
0.00%	Displays numbers as percentages with two decimal places.

Functions

A *function* is the action that Word performs on the values in a formula. Examples of functions are SUM, AVERAGE, and COUNT. The functions that you can use in a formula are listed in the **Formula** dialog box under the **Paste function** heading. The default function is SUM, which adds the numbers above or to the left of the formula.

You can delete everything from the **Formula** box and then enter a different function. Be sure to begin the formula with an equal sign. You can either type the function into the **Formula** box or select the function from the **Paste function** drop-down list. The examples in the table show some of the functions you might use.

Arguments

The *arguments* for a function are the entities within the parentheses following the function name in a formula. There are several types of arguments you can use in a function. For example, you can use the positional argument LEFT in the SUM function to have Word sum the values in all cells to the left of the cell that contains the formula.

Argument Type	Description	Examples
Numbers	The actual value to use in the computation	=SUM(3,5)
Positional arguments	Computes the values of numbers to the left, right, above, or below the current cell	LEFT, RIGHT, ABOVE, BELOW (and combinations of these positions) =PRODUCT(ABOVE,LEFT)
Bookmarks	Define a bookmark for a cell and then use the bookmark name in the formula	(Interest_rate,LEFT) where Interest_rate is the bookmark name of a cell containing a number
Cell references—RNCN	RNCN references where Rn refers to a row number and Cn refers to a column number	(R2C2) Refers to the second row, second column in the table
Cell references—A1	A1 references where the first column in a table is A and the first row is 1 (like in a Microsoft® Excel® spreadsheet)	(B3) Refers to the second column, third row (B3, C3) Refers to the second and third columns, third row (B2:C4) Refers to all of the cells from the second column, second row, through the third column, fourth row =AVERAGE(B2:B15)

> **Note:** All of the functions except FALSE require arguments. Refer to the Word Help topic "Use a formula in a Word table" for a description of all of the functions with examples.

Equations

An *equation* is a document element for adding complex mathematical symbols to your document. There are several predefined equations that you can insert into your document. You can also use the equation editor to create your own equations.

By default, the equations are formatted in professional format.

Professional format:

$$(1 + x)^n = 1 + \frac{nx}{1!} + \frac{n(n - 1)x^2}{2!} + \cdots$$

Figure 1-5: An equation in the professional format.

You can also format them in linear format.

Linear format:

$$(1 + x)^n = 1 + nx/1! + (n(n - 1) x^2)/2! + \cdots$$

Figure 1-6: An equation in the linear format.

Note: In Word Help, you can find additional information on creating and using equations.

Ink Equations

Word 2016 includes a new feature, Ink Equations, that enables you to input complex formulas by writing them with your mouse or a stylus. You create an ink equation by selecting the **Insert** tab and then, in the **Symbols** group, selecting **Equation→Ink Equation**. Word opens the **Ink Equation** dialog box, where you write the formula in the **Write math here** box. Word displays the typed equivalent to your formula above the **Write math here** box. When your formula is correct, select **Insert** to insert the formula into your document.

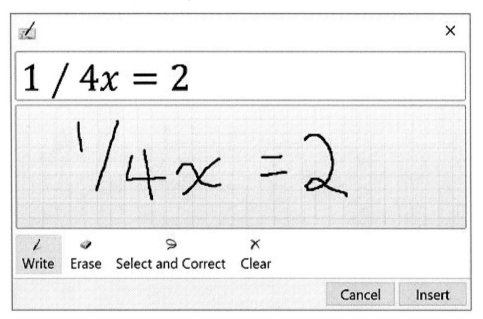

Figure 1-7: You can write your own equations in the Ink Equation dialog box.

Access the Checklist tile on your CHOICE Course screen for reference information and job aids on How to Perform Calculations in a Table.

ACTIVITY 1–3
Performing Calculations in a Table

Before You Begin
My Inventory.docx is open.

Scenario
You are reviewing the table your associate created to calculate the retail price of items. You notice that the items in the Appliances category do not contain the retail prices. You want to update the table without bothering your associate, so you examine the existing formulas so that you can enter the new formulas where needed.

---

1. Examine the formulas already in the table.
   a) Press **Alt+F9** to display the field codes. Examine the formula in the **Retail Price** cell for the Maple kitchen cabinets. This formula increases the wholesale price of the item by 10 percent.

Cabinets	Maple kitchen	$229.99	{ =SUM(LEFT)+(sum(left)*0.10)}	8

   b) Press **Alt+F9** again to toggle the field code display off.

2. Add a formula to the **Retail Price** cells for the **Dishwasher** item in the **Appliances** category.
   a) Select the cell in the **Retail Price** column to the right of the **Dishwasher** item.
   b) Select the **Table Tools Layout** tab.
   c) In the **Data** group, select **Formula**.
   d) In the **Formula** text box, modify the text so that it reads *=SUM(LEFT)+(SUM(LEFT)*.10)*

Formula	? ✕
Formula:	
=SUM(LEFT)+(SUM(LEFT)*.10)	
Number format:	
˅	
Paste function:	**Paste bookmark:**
˅	˅
	OK Cancel

 Note: Formulas in Word 2016 are not case sensitive.

e) Select **OK**. Word calculates the formula and displays the result in the cell. Press **Alt+F9** to toggle between the result and the formula.

Item Name	Wholesale Price	Retail Price
Dishwasher	$99.95	{ =SUM(LEFT)+(SUM(LEFT)*.1 0) }

3. Copy the formula for calculating the retail cost of the dishwasher to the other appliance items and calculate the results.
   a) If necessary, press **Alt+F9** to display the formula.
   b) Select the formula in the **Retail Price** cell for the **Dishwasher** item.
   c) Press **Ctrl+C** to copy the formula.
   d) Select the **Retail Price** cells for the remaining items in the **Appliances** category for which the retail price has not been calculated.
   e) Press **Ctrl+V** to paste the formula to all the **Appliances** items.
   f) Press **Alt+F9** to display the calculated values for the formulas.
      Notice that all **Appliances** items are displaying the same retail price as the dishwasher. By default, Word does not calculate the new values for each cell. You will need to select the value in each cell and press **F9** to have Word recalculate the results.
   g) Select all the values for the retail prices of appliances. Press **F9** to force Word to recalculate the formulas. You now see the correct retail price for each of the appliances.

HouSalvage Greene City Inventory				
Category	Item Name	Wholesale Price	Retail Price	Quantity on Hand
Appliances	Dishwasher	$99.95	$109.95	4
	Electric cooktop	$125.99	$138.59	2
	Electric front-loading washer	$119.99	$131.99	6
	Electric top-loading washer	$69.99	$76.99	3
	Electric water heater (50 gallons)	$139.99	$153.99	2
	Gas cooktop	$149.99	$164.99	7
	Gas water heater (50 gallons)	$159.99	$175.99	7
	Refrigerator side by side—25.4 cubic feet	$499.99	$549.99	3

4. Save and close the **My Inventory** file.
   a) Save your changes to the **My Inventory** file.
   b) Select **File→Close** to close the file and leave Word open.

TOPIC D

Create a Chart

You have worked with numerical data to perform calculations. You can also chart information to show relationships between values, show trends, and summarize information in a graphical way. Showing table data in a chart can help your audience more easily understand the information.

Charts

A *chart* is a graphical interpretation of data. The information can be organized as points on a line, grouped into columns or bars, or shown as slices in a circle or a pie. Line and bar charts have a vertical and a horizontal axis with a scale showing the values on one axis and labels describing the data on the other axis. All types of charts should have a title. Pie charts use a legend to indicate what each color in the chart represents.

Chart Components

A chart is composed of several components. Some components are displayed by default, and others you can add if necessary. Some chart components can be moved, resized, or reformatted.

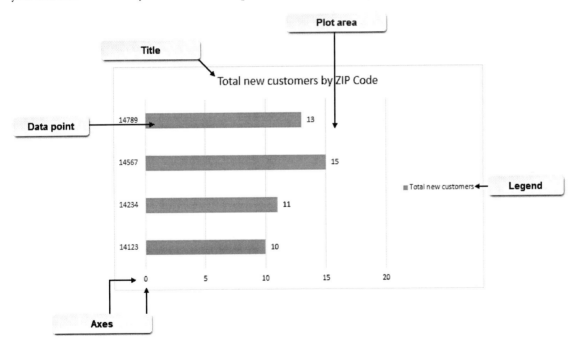

Figure 1–8: Chart components as seen in a bar chart.

The following table describes each component of a chart.

Chart Component	Description
Chart area	The entire chart and all chart components.
Plot area	The area inside the two axes where the data series are located.
Axis	There are two axes. The vertical, or y-axis, usually contains data. The horizontal, or x-axis, usually contains categories. These can be reversed, as shown in the preceding figure.

Chart Component	Description
Title	Text to describe the chart. It can be aligned with an axis or centered above the chart.
Data label	Labels can be added to provide additional information, such as showing the actual value of a bar on a bar chart inside the bar.

Types of Charts

Several types of charts are available in Word. Different types of charts display data in different ways. Some types of charts are more appropriate for displaying your data than other charts, depending on the type of data you are charting and what you want your audience to learn from your data.

Chart Type	Description
Column	Useful for comparing data or showing changes over time.
Line	Useful for showing trends over a period of time.
Pie	Useful for charting a single column or row of data. It shows the size of each item in relation to the total of all data.
Bar	Useful for comparing data. The x-axis is the vertical axis and the y-axis is the horizontal axis in a bar chart.
Area	Useful for showing the magnitude of change over time and to illustrate the total value in a trend.
XY (Scatter)	Useful for showing relationships between numeric values in several data series. It also can be used to graph two groups of numbers as a single series of XY coordinates.
Stock	Useful for displaying the fluctuation in data such as stock market prices or scientific data.
Surface	Useful for finding favorable patterns among set data sets.
Radar	Useful for comparing the aggregate values of multiple data series.
Combo	Uses a combination of chart types to represent data. Useful for comparing multiple data series.

Note: For more information, check out LearnTO **Determine Which Chart Type to Use** from the **LearnTO** tile on your CHOICE Course screen.

The Chart in Microsoft Word Window

When you add a chart to your Word document, the **Chart in Microsoft Word** window opens. This is an actual instance of Microsoft Excel that opens with sample data already displayed. You can copy data from your Word document or manually enter data in the spreadsheet to be graphed. By default, the **Chart in Microsoft Word** window has four rows and three columns for your data. If you paste data that doesn't consist of as many columns and/or rows, you must delete the extra data in order for Word to chart your data properly. When you close the window, the chart is added to your document at the location where your cursor was when you chose to insert the chart.

	A	B	C	D
1		Series 1	Series 2	Series 3
2	Category 1	4.3	2.4	2
3	Category 2	2.5	4.4	2
4	Category 3	3.5	1.8	3
5	Category 4	4.5	2.8	5

Figure 1-9: Use the Chart in Microsoft Word window to define the data you want to graph.

Note: If Microsoft Excel is not installed on your computer, when you create a data chart, Microsoft Graph opens instead of Excel. You cannot use advanced data charting functions without Microsoft Excel installed.

Chart Tools

After you create a chart, you can make changes to the design, layout, and format of the chart from the **Chart Tools Design** and **Chart Tools Format** contextual tabs in Word. Select the chart to display these contextual tabs.

The **Chart Tools Design** tab enables you to:

- Add chart elements.
- Apply a **Quick Layout**.
- Select a predefined chart style.
- Switch the rows with the columns.
- Select, edit, or refresh data.
- Select a predefined chart layout.
- Change the chart type.

The **Chart Tools Format** tab enables you to:

- Format the current selection.
- Reset the current selection to match the selected style.
- Insert and configure shape styles, including selecting predefined styles, shape fill, shape outline, and shape effects.
- Configure WordArt styles, including adding WordArt, text fill, text outline, and text effects.
- Arrange the chart position and *text wrap* options.
- Specify a specific height and width for the chart.

Chart Buttons

When you select a chart, four small buttons are displayed to the upper-right corner of the chart. You can use these buttons as an alternative to selecting configuration options from the ribbon.

Button	Options	Description
Layout Options ⌃	• **In Line with Text** • **With Text Wrapping** • **Move with text** • **Fix position on page**	Choose how your chart interacts with the text around it.

Button	Options	Description
Chart Elements ✛	• **Axes** • **Axis Titles** • **Chart Title** • **Data Labels** • **Data Table** • **Error Bars** • **Gridlines** • **Legend** • **Trendline**	Add, remove, or change chart elements.
Chart Styles 🖌	• **Style** • **Color**	Set the style and color scheme for the chart.

Chart Filters ▼	• **Values**
	    • **Series**
	    • **Categories**
	 • **Names**
	    • **Series**
	    • **Categories**
		Specify which data points and names are included in the chart.

The Caption Dialog Box

You might want to add a caption to your chart. This places a caption in your document above or below the chart. From the **Caption** dialog box, you can specify caption details such as the caption text, the type of label for the caption, and the caption location. The default label types do not include charts, so if you have multiple charts you would like to number and caption, you will want to add a new label type for charts.

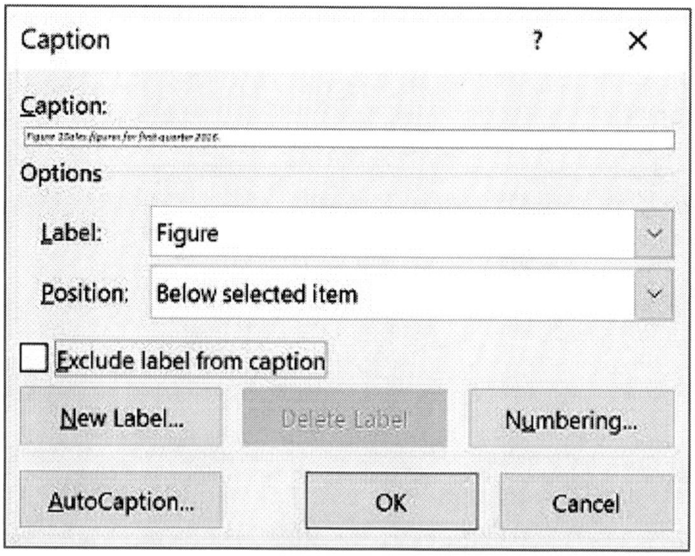

Figure 1–10: Use the Caption dialog box to add a caption below a chart.

Access the Checklist tile on your CHOICE Course screen for reference information and job aids on **How to Create a Chart.**

ACTIVITY 1–4
Creating a Chart

Data File

Desktop\Building with Heart\Organizing Content Using Tables and Charts\Building with Heart - Brochure.docx

Before You Begin

For this activity to work as written, you must have Microsoft Excel installed. If it is not installed, some steps might be different because you will be working in Microsoft Graph instead of Excel.

Scenario

Building with Heart is updating their brochure that they mail out to prospective donors. Currently, the brochure has a table that indicates the increase in need compared to the increase in funding for regions within Greene City. You would like to increase the visual appeal of the brochure by adding a chart to illustrate the table's contents.

1. Open the **Building with Heart - Brochure.docx** document.
   a) In the **Desktop\Building with Heart\Organizing Content Using Tables and Charts** folder, open the **Building with Heart - Brochure** document.
   b) Save the file as *My Building with Heart - Brochure*

2. Copy the data in the table below the heading "The Need" and insert a chart.
   a) Scroll to the bottom of page 1 and select all the rows and columns in the table below **The Need**.

Region	Increase in Need	Increase in Funding
Eastern King County	12.45%	2.2%
Northern King County and 4th Ward	6.7%	3.2%
Downtown and 12th Ward	3.32%	0.005%
Western King County	2.6%	1.12%

   b) Press **Ctrl+C** to copy the data to the clipboard.
   c) Position the cursor at the beginning of the **Who Can Volunteer** heading.
   d) On the **Insert** tab, in the **Illustrations** group, select **Chart**.
   e) In the **Insert Chart** dialog box, select the various chart types to see examples of the available chart types.
   f) In the list under **All Charts**, select **Column**.
   g) On the right side of the **Insert Chart** dialog box, select the first column chart (**Clustered Column**) to create a bar chart.
   h) Select **OK**. The **Chart in Microsoft Word** window opens with sample data. If necessary, resize the **Chart in Microsoft Word** window so that you can view the data.

i) Select cell **A1** and then press **Ctrl+V** to paste the data you copied from Word into the spreadsheet.

	A	B	C
1	Region	Increase in Need	Increase in Funding
2	Eastern King County	12.45%	2.20%
3	Northern King County and 4th Ward	6.70%	3.20%
4	Downtown and 12th Ward	3.32%	0.01%
5	Western King County	2.60%	1.12%
6			

Chart in Microsoft Word

j) Notice that the **Chart in Microsoft Word** window still contains the sample column with the **Series 3** heading. You must delete this column in order for Word to display your chart correctly.

k) In the **Chart in Microsoft Word** window, select the sample data in column D, rows 1 through 5. Right-click and select **Delete** and then select **Table Columns** to delete the unneeded sample data.

l) Close the **Chart in Microsoft Word** window.

m) Observe the chart that Word inserted into the brochure.

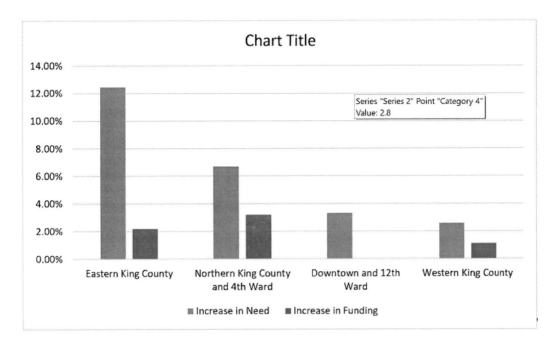

By default, Word inserted the chart at the top of page 2. Word automatically created a chart legend to identify the **Increase in Need** and **Increase in Funding** items. It also added a placeholder for the chart title, and configured the chart so that text wraps around it (notice that the "Who Can Volunteer" heading appears to the right of the chart).

3. Change the chart type and add data labels.

   a) On the **Chart Tools Design** tab, in the **Type** group, select **Change Chart Type**.

   b) With **Column** selected, select **3-D Clustered Column** and then select **OK**.

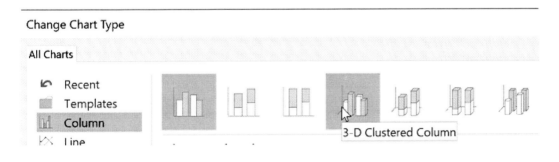

   c) With the chart selected, select the **Chart Elements** button. +

    d) Check **Data Labels**. Word adds numbers to the top of the columns in the chart to identify their values.

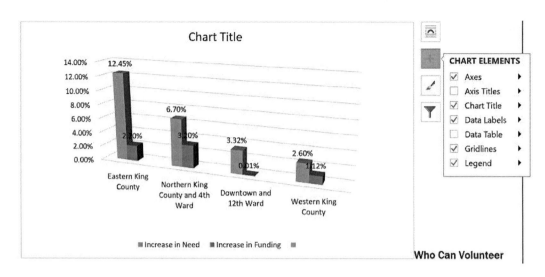

4. Add a chart title.

    a) In the new chart, click once to select the **Chart Title** text box and then select the text within the box.

    b) Type *The Need for Affordable Housing by Region* for the title.

    c) Select the chart again to deselect the chart title.

5. Change the chart style and manage text wrapping.

    a) On the **Chart Tools Design** tab, in the **Chart Styles** group, select the **Style 8** chart style or another chart style of your choice.

    b) By the upper-right corner of the chart, select the **Layout Options** button.

c) On the **Layout Options** palette, select **Top and Bottom** so that the text appears above and below the chart, not beside it.

The "Who Can Volunteer" heading now appears below the chart instead of beside it.

d) Close the **Layout Options** palette.

6. Save the file and close it.

TOPIC E

Add an Excel Table to a Word Document (Optional)

Imagine you need to create a sales report that contains both paragraphs of text along with sales information from an Excel workbook. Word has the ability to handle simple calculations in a table, but it is not capable of handling complex formulas. Likewise, although Excel is the premier application for presenting columns and rows of data, it is not designed to work as a word processor. In this scenario, your best choice is to type your report in a Word document and then add the information from the Excel workbook to the Word document.

Excel Data in a Word Document

As you have seen in this lesson, Word 2016 enables you to create and format tables and even perform calculations on the data within tables. But if you need to perform complex calculations or have a large amount of data, you will need the power of a worksheet program like Excel 2016. The good news is that even if you create a table in Excel, you can still copy and paste its information into Word. Further, through a process referred to as *linking*, you can paste and link an Excel table within a Word document so that any new changes you make to the Excel table are automatically reflected in the linked table within Word.

When you paste an Excel table into Word, Word enables you to choose how you paste that table. The following table describes your options.

Paste Button	Description
Keep Source Formatting	This option pastes the Excel table into Word as a Word table. If you later change the Excel table, the Word table will not be updated. This option keeps the formatting you applied in Excel on the table in Word.
Use Destination Styles	Use this option to paste the Excel table into a Word table and remove the formatting you applied in Excel. This option enables you to apply any of the Word table styles to the copy of the Excel table in Word. Note that if you later change the Excel table, Word will not update the Word table with your changes.
Link & Keep Source Formatting	Use this option to link a copy of the Excel table into your Word document and keep the Excel formatting. By linking the table, you enable Word to update the table whenever you make changes to the Excel table.

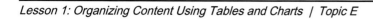

Paste Button	Description
Link & Use Destination Styles	This option links a copy of the Excel table in your Word document and removes the Excel formatting. Linking the table enables Word to update the contents of the table whenever you modify the Excel table.
Picture	Use this option to paste a snapshot of the table as a graphic instead of a Word table. Pasting the table as a graphic enables you to resize and wrap text around it just like you would a photo. Any subsequent changes you make to the original Excel table will not be reflected in this snapshot of the table in Word.
Keep Text Only	You use this option when you want just a copy of the contents of the Excel table without any table formatting in Word. Keep in mind that any changes you make to the Excel table will not be updated in the Word copy of it.

The Object Dialog Box

Another option you can use to insert an Excel table into a Word document is the **Insert Object** dialog box. This dialog box enables you to create an object such as an Excel table within a Word document. Alternatively, you can use the **Insert Object** dialog box to link an existing file (again, such as an Excel workbook) within a Word document. When you insert an existing file, you can check the **Link to file** check box so that Word will automatically update the object whenever you modify the source file. Whether you create a new object or use an existing file, you can check the **Display as icon** check box to configure Word to display the object as a clickable icon within your document rather than the contents of the file. You open the **Insert Object** dialog box by selecting the **Insert** tab and then, in the **Text** group, selecting **Object**.

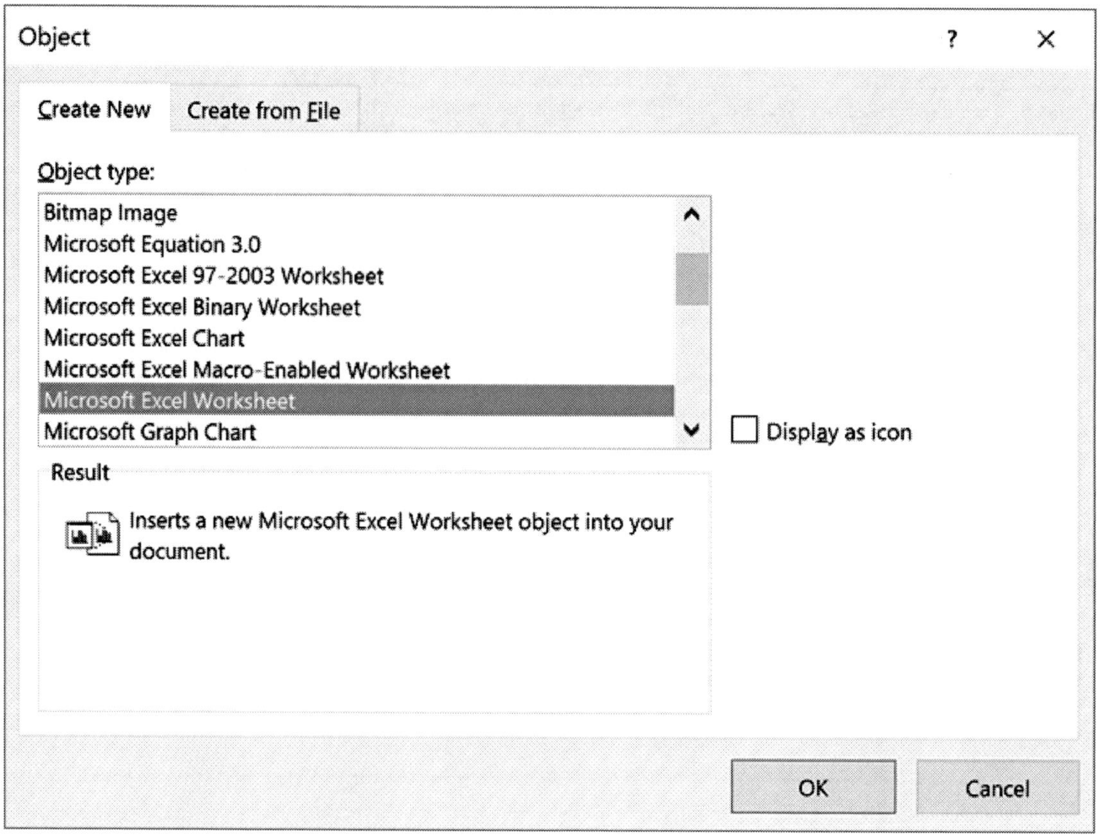

Figure 1-11: The Object dialog box.

You can use the **Insert Object** dialog box to create or insert data from files created by a variety of programs, not just Excel. Other supported document types include:

- Adobe® Acrobat® PDFs
- Bitmap images
- PowerPoint® presentations
- WordPad documents

After you insert an object into a Word document, selecting that object results in Word displaying the interface for the type of object. For example, if you use the **Insert Object** dialog box to insert an Excel worksheet into your Word document, when you select the Excel table, Word displays the Excel ribbon, gridlines, column and row headings, and so on.

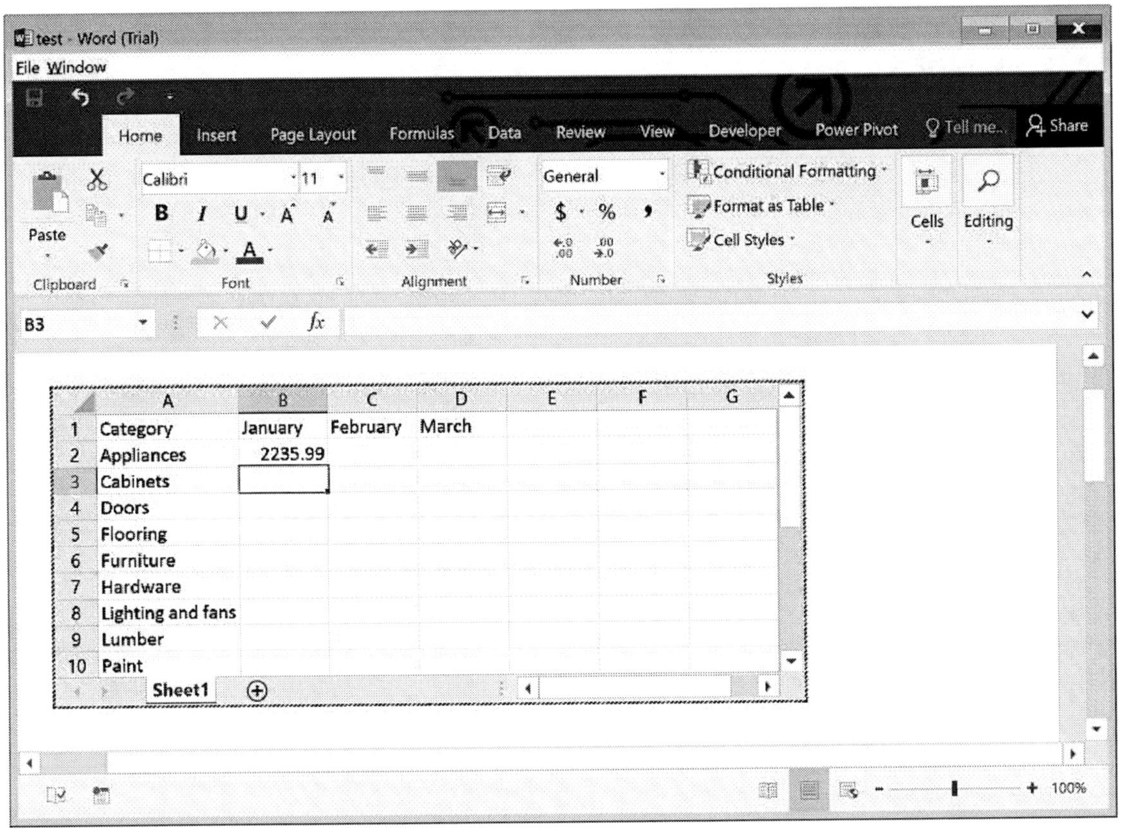

Figure 1-12: The Excel interface in Word.

Access the Checklist tile on your CHOICE Course screen for reference information and job aids on How to Add an Excel Table to a Word Document.

ACTIVITY 1–5
Adding an Excel Table to a Word Document

Data Files

Desktop\Building with Heart\Organizing Content Using Tables and Charts\HouSalvage First Quarter Sales Report.docx

Desktop\Building with Heart\Organizing Content Using Tables and Charts\HouSalvage First Quarter Sales Report - Greene City.xlsx

Scenario

You are responsible for preparing the sales report for HouSalvage Greene City for the first quarter. You have prepared a Word document with analysis of the quarter's sales. You also have an Excel workbook that contains the sales for each category of items HouSalvage sells for each month of the quarter. You want to include the information contained in the Excel workbook in your sales report in Word. You aren't sure whether the sales numbers in the Excel workbook are final, so you want to make sure that any changes made to the Excel workbook will be reflected in your sales report in Word.

---

1. Open the **HouSalvage First Quarter Sales Report.docx** document.

   a) In the **Desktop\Building with Heart\Organizing Content Using Tables and Charts** folder, open the **HouSalvage First Quarter Sales Report.docx** document.
   This file opens in Word.

   b) Save the file as *My HouSalvage First Quarter Sales Report.docx*

2. Open the **HouSalvage First Quarter Sales Report - Greene City.xlsx** document.

   a) In the **Desktop\Building with Heart\Organizing Content Using Tables and Charts** folder, open the **HouSalvage First Quarter Sales Report - Greene City.xlsx** document.
   This file opens in Excel.

   b) Observe the workbook.
   The table in the workbook contains the sales for each category of item that HouSalvage stocks (such as appliances, cabinets, and so on). The sales are for each of the months in the first quarter. The table also shows the total sales for each category of item and the percentage of total sales each category represents.

   c) In Excel, select **File→Save As**.

   d) Below **Current Folder**, select the **Organizing Content Using Tables and Charts** folder.

   e) In the **File name** text box, type *My HouSalvage First Quarter Sales Report - Greene City* and then select **Save**.

3. Copy the sales information in Excel.

a) In Excel, select cells **A8** through **F20**.

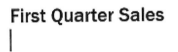

Category	January	February	March	Total Sales by Category	Percentage of Total Sales
Appliances	2,235.99	3,189.79	2,497.35	$7,923.13	13%
Cabinets	895.15	2,175.49	1,378.45	$4,449.09	7%
Doors	959.99	459.99	1,155.29	$2,575.27	4%
Flooring	4,375.85	3,765.41	4,495.59	$12,636.85	21%
Furniture	1,589.25	1,149.29	1,278.89	$4,017.43	7%
Hardware	565.49	747.65	699.99	$2,013.13	3%
Lighting and Fans	1,378.59	1,498.45	1,759.25	$4,636.29	8%
Lumber	3,789.29	4,139.25	3,965.27	$11,893.81	20%
Paint	789.50	989.27	835.29	$2,614.06	4%
Plumbing	659.25	751.49	709.50	$2,120.24	4%
Windows	931.75	1,987.65	1,625.39	$4,544.79	8%
Total Monthly Sales	$18,170.10	$20,853.73	$20,400.26	$59,424.09	100%

b) Press **Ctrl+C** to copy the table to the clipboard.

4. In Word, paste the table.
   a) In Word, click the line below the heading **First Quarter Sales**.

First Quarter Sales

|

   b) Right-click and observe the **Paste Options** on the shortcut menu.

Word offers six options for pasting the Excel table into your document:
- Keep Source Formatting
- Use Destination Styles
- Link & Use Destination Styles
- Link & Keep Source Formatting
- Picture
- Keep Text Only

   c) Below **Paste Options**, select **Keep Source Formatting**.
   This option pastes a copy of the Excel table as a table but does not link it to the original Excel workbook. This means that if you change the data in Excel, you won't see the change reflected in the copy of the table in Word.
   d) On the **Quick Access Toolbar**, select **Undo** to undo the paste of the table as a Word table.

   e) Below the heading **First Quarter Sales**, right-click and select **Link & Keep Source Formatting**.
   Pasting the table using **Link & Keep Source Formatting** links the table in the Word document to the Excel workbook. This means that any changes you make in the Excel workbook will be reflected in the Word document.

5. Change the March sales for the Appliances category to 2,697.35.
   a) In Excel, select cell **D9**.
   This cell contains the **March** sales for the **Appliances** category.
   b) Enter *2697.35*

c) Save the **Excel** file.

d) Switch to Word. Observe the **March** sales for the **Appliances** category. Notice that Word has not updated the value.

You must use the **Update Link** command for Word to update the linked table with the current sales information.

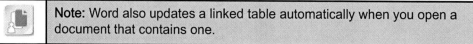

> **Note:** Word also updates a linked table automatically when you open a document that contains one.

e) Right-click in the sales table and select **Update Link**. Click elsewhere in the Word document to deselect the table.

✂ Cut
📋 Copy
📋 **Paste Options:**
📋
📋 Update Link
Linked Worksheet Object ▸
A Font...
🔳 Paragraph...

You now see that the sales of appliances were $2,697.35 in March.

6. Save and close the files.

a) In Word, save the **My HouSalvage First Quarter Sales Report** document and close Word.

b) Close Excel.

Summary

In this lesson, you worked with tables and charts. You organized the data in the tables to make it informative and visually appealing. You made information meaningful by sorting the data, merging cells, and performing calculations. Adding a chart summarized the information in the table to show the information in a graphical way. You also learned how to insert an Excel worksheet into a Word document.

What types of data might you put into a table that you would perform calculations on, and what types of calculations might you perform?

Will you be charting table data in your documents and, if so, what types of charts will you use?

Note: Check your CHOICE Course screen for opportunities to interact with your classmates, peers, and the larger CHOICE online community about the topics covered in this course or other topics you are interested in. From the Course screen you can also access available resources for a more continuous learning experience.

2 | Customizing Formats Using Styles and Themes

Lesson Time: 45 minutes

Lesson Objectives

In this lesson, you will customize formats using styles and themes. You will:

- Create and modify custom text styles.
- Create custom list and table styles.
- Apply document themes.

Lesson Introduction

An organization should have a standard look and feel for their documents both inside and outside the organization. Formatting documents using styles and themes helps define the organization's identity. Using styles and themes helps you maintain a consistent look and feel in your documents. In this lesson, you will customize the look of text within a newsletter through the use of styles and themes.

TOPIC A

Create and Modify Text Styles

As you become more proficient with Microsoft® Word, you might find you want to give your documents a more polished and professional appearance. One strategy you can use to give your documents a more polished look is to use styles for text in your document. In this topic, you will use various character and paragraph formatting options to create a custom style.

The fonts and formatting within your document should be consistent with the look and feel your organizational guidelines define. To help ensure that you are using the proper fonts and formatting, you can create styles that define such things as font size and color, and paragraph spacing and alignment. You can store these settings in a style that you can then use in your documents to maintain consistency.

Types of Text Styles

Word includes built-in styles, and you can create your own. A *style* is a set of one or more formatting characteristics. The formatting characteristics might include the font name, font size, font color, paragraph alignment and spacing, borders, or shading. The built-in styles that come with Word include the **Heading** styles, which are paragraph styles. There are also character styles such as the **Emphasis** and **Strong** styles. Some styles are linked, meaning they contain character and paragraph formatting that you can apply to selected text.

One of the time-saving features of styles is that if you change the formatting of a style, Word automatically updates all of the text to which you have applied that style to the new style formatting.

Title
Subtitle – Some of the built-in styles

Heading 1
This is the Normal paragraph style. You can apply *Emphasis* as well as *Intense Emphasis*. **Strong** is another character style.

Heading 2
Pressing Enter after creating a Heading puts the paragraph into the Normal paragraph style.

Heading 3
Notice how each Heading style has a similar look but uses a different paragraph formatting.

Figure 2–1: Built-in style examples.

You can select styles on the **Home** tab, in the **Styles** group. Examples of the styles are shown in the **Styles** gallery.

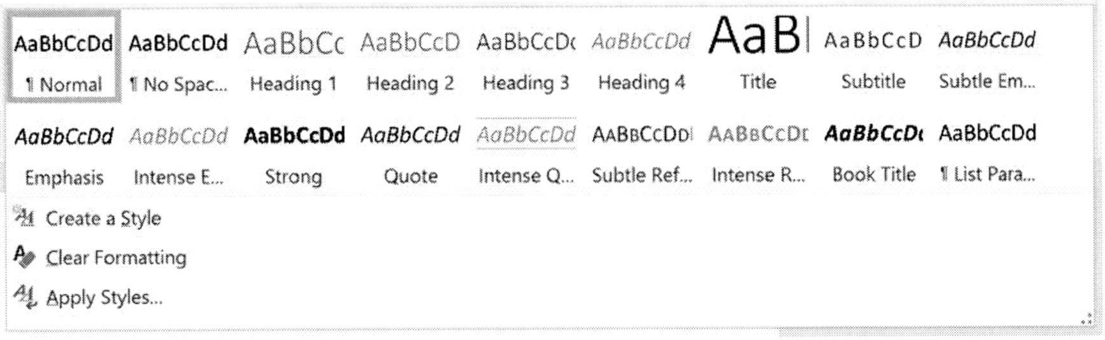

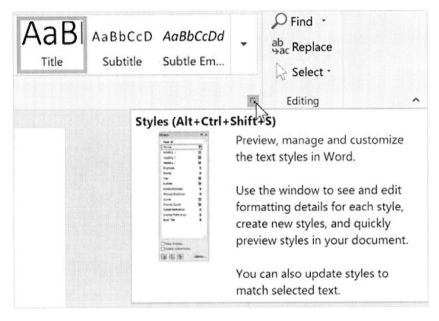

Figure 2-2: Styles on the Home tab show example text.

Select the **Styles** Dialog Box Launcher in the corner of the **Styles** group to display a floating **Styles** task pane. You can position the task pane anywhere on the screen so that it is available no matter which tab you have activated in Word.

Figure 2-3: Launch the Styles task pane from the Dialog Box Launcher in the corner of the Styles group.

You can see a list of the styles and whether they are character, paragraph, or linked styles in the **Styles** task pane. The character styles show an "a" in the right column, the paragraph styles show a paragraph marker in the right column, and linked styles show both.

To see what each of the styles looks like in the **Styles** pane before applying the style, check **Show Preview** at the bottom of the **Styles** task pane. The style name is then displayed in the defined style.

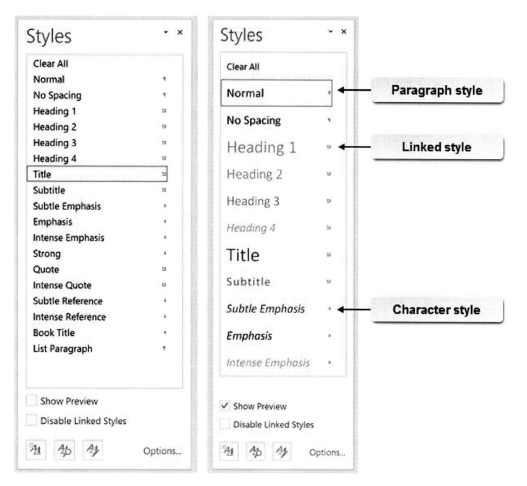

Figure 2-4: The Styles task pane with and without Show Preview.

Character Style

Character styles define the formatting you apply to text. This includes the font name, font size, color of the text, and the font style (bold, underline, italic, strikethrough); text effects and borders; and character spacing. Select the text you want to format in a particular style and then select the desired character style. The built-in styles **Emphasis**, **Subtle Emphasis**, and **Intense Emphasis** are examples of character styles.

Character styles do not format the line spacing, indentation, or text alignment.

Paragraph Style

A *paragraph style* formats paragraph appearance as well as all of the formatting included in character styles. Paragraph styles include the alignment of the text within the paragraph, tab stops, line spacing, and borders. The paragraph style applies to the entire paragraph. The built-in styles **Normal** and **No Spacing** are examples of paragraph styles.

Linked Style

A *linked style* contains both character and paragraph formatting. You can apply it to a word, to multiple words, or to a paragraph. If you apply it to text within a paragraph, then Word applies only the character formatting. If you click in a paragraph without selecting any text or if you select one or more paragraphs, then Word applies the paragraph formatting. The built-in styles **Heading 1**, **Heading 2**, **Title**, and **Subtitle** are examples of linked styles.

You can use linked styles to format the beginning of a paragraph with the same style as the headings in your document. This is referred to as a run-in or side head.

> Heading
>
> This is an example of a run-in head. Notice how the formatting of the Heading above this paragraph has the same formatting as the first two words of this paragraph. This was accomplished by using the linked style Heading 1 in both instances.

Figure 2-5: A linked style used as a paragraph style and a character style on "Heading" and "This is."

Heading and Subheading Styles

Headings can also make browsing a document easier. Word automatically lists text to which you apply a **Heading** style in the **Navigation** pane. From here, you can select the heading to go to where that heading is in the document. Different levels of **Heading** styles are also formatted for easy navigation.

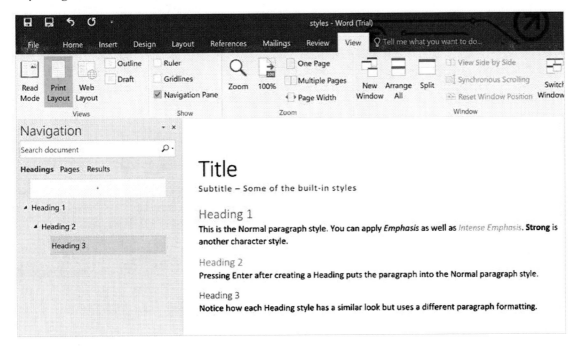

Figure 2-6: Heading and Subheading styles are added to the Navigation pane.

Character Spacing

In the **Font** dialog box, you can change the *character spacing*. Character spacing formatting enables you to control the size of characters and the space between characters. You can specify that the selected text be scaled up or down from the current size, condense or expand the spacing between characters, and raise or lower the position of the characters.

Kerning

You can also enable *kerning* for large fonts to adjust spacing between specific letter pairs so that the spacing appears even. Kerning applies to specific pairs of characters when they occur together. Not all fonts include kerning data, so Word might not apply kerning even if you enable it. An example of two letters in which Word would apply kerning would be "aw" in the word "awesome." With kerning, the bottom of the "a" is pushed under the top of the "w" so that they appear closer together. The other letters in the word "awesome" would not be affected by the kerning since there would be no need to adjust their spacing to make them appear evenly spaced.

Figure 2-7: Examples of large text with and without kerning enabled.

Custom Styles

If none of the built-in styles meet your needs, you can create your own *custom styles*. For a custom style, you set the formatting for the characters or paragraphs and then save the style with a unique name. You can create a custom style from scratch or base it on an existing style. After formatting text with the desired attributes, select the text, right-click, and from the **Mini** toolbar, select **Styles→Create New Style**. This displays the **Create New Style from Formatting** dialog box. You can also select the **New Style** button in the **Styles** task pane to display the **Create New Style from Formatting** dialog box.

 Note: For more information, check out LearnTO **Assign Keyboard Shortcuts to Styles** from the **LearnTO** tile on your CHOICE Course screen.

The Normal Template

By default, Word automatically opens a file in the background that contains the built-in styles whenever you create a new document. Microsoft calls this background file the Normal template. When you create a custom style, you can choose to store the styles in the Normal template. Doing so makes the custom styles available to you whenever you create a new document.

Word stores the Normal template in the C:\Users*username*\AppData\Roaming\Microsoft \Templates folder. By default, the C:\Users*username*\AppData folder, its contents, and all subfolders are hidden in Windows® 10. The file name of the Normal template is Normal.dotm.

The Create New Style from Formatting Dialog Box

When you create a new style, the **Create New Style from Formatting** dialog box is displayed. Through the options in this dialog box, you can configure the settings for the new style.

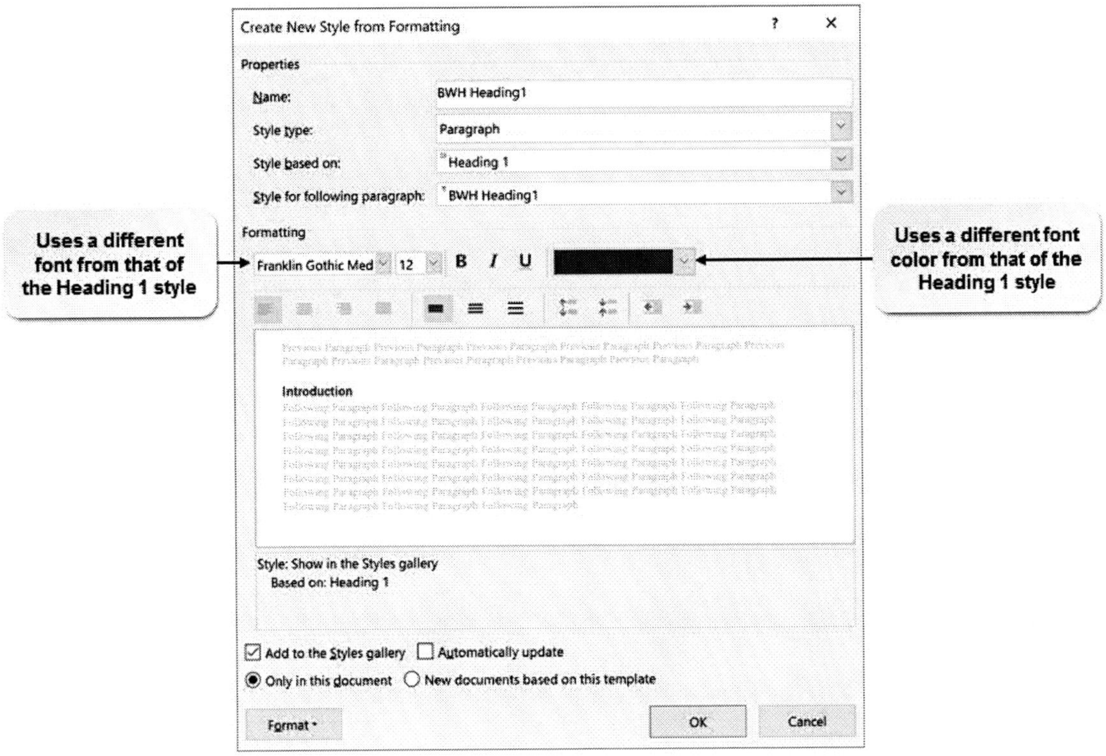

Figure 2-8: The Create New Style from Formatting dialog box.

The following table describes the options in the **Create New Style from Formatting** dialog box.

Set This	To
Name	Specify the name for the new style.
Style type	Specify whether the style is a character, paragraph, linked, list, or table style.
Style for following paragraph	Specify the paragraph style that is applied to the paragraph after the paragraph where you apply this style.
Formatting	Specify formatting options for the style type. • **Characters**: Font, font size, font attributes, font color • **Paragraph**: Alignment, spacing, indents • **Table**: Line style, line thickness, borders, shading • **Lists**: Numbering or bullet style, indent levels
Preview area	See the settings in sample text.
Add to the Styles gallery	Add the new character or paragraph style to the **Styles** gallery.
Automatically update	Automatically update the paragraph style when a change is made to any paragraph with that style applied, and propagate the updated style to any other paragraphs formatted with that style.
Only in this document	Make the style available in the current document only.
New documents based on this template	Make the style available to any documents you create that are based on the Normal template or the template you are currently using.

Set This	To
Format	Set additional formatting options for **Fonts, Paragraphs, Tabs, Borders, Language, Frame, Numbering, Shortcut Key,** and **Text Effects**.

Style Modification Options

There are times you might find you need to modify the styles in your documents. You can modify the text in your document and then apply that change to the style, or you can modify the style directly. A style modification applies the changes to any text to which you have applied that style.

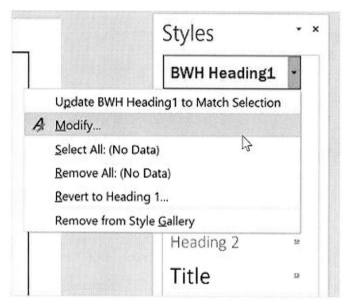

Figure 2–9: Modify a style from the Styles pane.

Style Sets

Word includes several sets of styles that are designed to work together. From the **Design** tab, you can change the style set that you are using. Select the down arrow in the lower-left corner of the **Style Set** box.

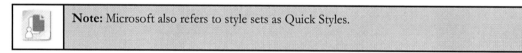

Note: Microsoft also refers to style sets as Quick Styles.

This Document

Title

Heading 1

On the Insert tab, the galleries include items that are designed to coordinate with the overall look of your document. You can use these galleries to insert tables, headers, footers, lists, cover pages,

Built-In

TITLE	Title	Title	TITLE	Title	Title
Heading 1	Heading 1	Heading 1	HEADING 1	HEADING 1	1 HEADING 1

Title	Title	Title
Heading 1	Heading 1	Heading 1

Reset to the Default Style Set

Save as a New Style Set...

Figure 2-10: You can change which style set you use if you want a different set of styles to select from.

Custom Style Sets

Word 2016 enables you to create your own custom style sets. To create a custom style set, format a title, heading, and normal paragraph text with the font settings (such as type, color, and size) as you would like the style set to contain. Select the text, and then on the **Design** tab in the **Document Formatting** group, select the **More** button to display the list of style sets. Next, select **Save as a New Style Set**. By default, Word stores the style set in a template file in the hidden folder **C: \Users*username*\AppData\Roaming\Microsoft\QuickStyles**. After you save a custom style set, Word includes it in the style set gallery below the heading **Custom**.

If you want to share your custom style sets with other users, you must copy the template file from the hidden folder **C:\Users*username*\AppData\Roaming\Microsoft\QuickStyles** to the equivalent folder on the other users' computers. Remember, you can configure **File Explorer** to display hidden files by selecting the **View** tab, and in the **Show/hide** group, selecting the **Hidden items** check box.

Body and Heading Styles

You might have noticed that there is a **Body** style and a **Heading** style as well as a **+Body** font and a **+Headings** font. Setting the **+Body** and **+Headings** fonts enables you to select the font by selecting a theme. If you want to set the default font style and size, in the **Font** dialog box, set the desired font attributes for **+Body** and **+Headings**, then select **Set As Default**.

When you select one of the themes—either one of the supplied themes or one you create—the style in the **Body Text** and **Heading** *N* (where *N* is 1 through 9) is applied as defined in the theme.

> Access the Checklist tile on your CHOICE Course screen for reference information and job aids on **How to Create and Modify Text Styles**.

ACTIVITY 2-1
Creating and Modifying Text Styles

Data File

Desktop\Building with Heart\Customizing Formats Using Styles and Themes\New store flyer.docx

Scenario

The director of Building with Heart provided you with the basic information for a flyer that will go out to customers of its HouSalvage stores. The director asked you to modify this flyer for next month when another store opens. To save time on the new flyer, you decide to use styles to maintain consistency between the flyers and use the same formatting on both flyers.

---

1. Open the **New store flyer.docx** file and save it with a new name.
   a) In the **Desktop\Building with Heart\Customizing Formats Using Styles and Themes** folder, open **New store flyer.docx**.
   b) Save the file as *My new store flyer.docx*

2. Use the built-in **Title** style to format the HouSalvage Recycling Centers store name.
   a) In My new store flyer.docx, click in the first line of text (that reads "HouSalvage Recycling Centers").
   b) On the **Home** tab, in the **Styles** group, hover over several different styles and notice that Word applies a live preview of each style to the text.
   c) Select **Title**.

3. Apply the **Subtitle** style to format the tagline.
   a) Click in the second line of text (that begins with "Your source for...").
   b) On the **Home** tab, in the **Styles** group, select **Subtitle**.

4. Apply the **Strong** style to the word "new."
   a) Select the word **new** in the first full paragraph.
   b) On the **Home** tab, in the **Styles** group, in the **Styles** drop-down list, select **Strong**.

5. Create a new style based on the **Title** style, changing the title to a red font and centering it.
   a) In the lower-right corner of the **Styles** group, select the **Styles** Dialog Box Launcher to display the **Styles** task pane.
   b) Select the text at the top of the document that you formatted with the **Title** style.
   c) In the **Styles** task pane, select **New Style**. The **Create New Style from Formatting** dialog box opens.
   d) In the **Name** text box, type *Store Name*
   e) Under the **Formatting** section, change the font to **Arial Black, 24 point, Bold, Red,** and **Center aligned.**
   f) Select **OK**.

6. Create a new style based on the **Subtitle** style.
   a) Select the text **Your source for recycled construction materials since 1995**.
   b) In the **Styles** pane, select **New Style**.
   c) Name the new style *Tagline* and base it on the **Subtitle** style. Use the attributes **Arial, 14 point, Italic, Red, centered**.
   d) Select **OK**.

7. Create a **Flyer Text** style.
   a) Select the text **You have been a loyal customer**.
   b) In the **Styles** pane, select **New Style**.
   c) Base the new style on the **Normal** style and name it *Flyer Text*. Set the attributes to **Arial**, **11 point**.
   d) Select **OK**.
   e) Apply the **Flyer Text** style to everything from "Dear Customer" down through "Linda Bell, Director."

8. Apply character spacing to emphasize the text "8:00 AM next Saturday."
   a) In the third full paragraph, select the text **8:00 AM next Saturday**.
   b) Right-click the selected text and select **Font**.
   c) Select the **Advanced** tab.
   d) From the **Scale** drop-down list, select **150%**.

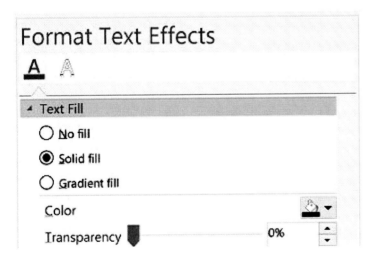

   e) Select **Text Effects**.
   f) Expand **Text Fill**.

   g) Verify that **Solid fill** is selected, and from the **Color** drop-down list, select **Red**.
   h) Below **Format Text Effects**, select **Text Effects**.

i)   Expand **Shadow**.

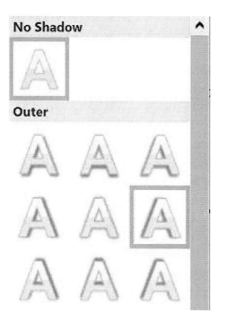

j)   From the **Presets** drop-down list, in the **Outer** group, select **Offset Left**.

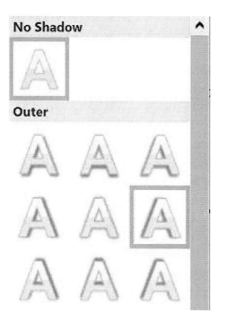

k)   Select **OK** twice.

l) Verify that your document looks like the following example.

HouSalvage Recycle Centers

Your source for recycled construction materials since 1995

Dear Customer,

We are opening a **new** store near you! We are having a grand opening sale and hope to see you there.

You have been a loyal customer and we hope this makes your shopping experience with us even better. We noticed how long the lines are getting at our current HouSalvage stores and how often we are running out of stock with no room in the back to store any additional items. It seemed the logical choice to open a new store. We liked the idea so much that we are opening two new stores!

The ribbon cutting ceremony will take place **at 8:00 AM next Saturday** for our South Greene store located at 84 River Road. Next month, we will open our Riverside location at 35 North Maple Avenue.

There will be free balloons, popcorn, and discounts galore. Bring this flyer in and save an additional 15% on your purchase.

Thank you for being a loyal customer!

Sincerely,

Linda Bell, Director

m) Save the file in the current folder.

TOPIC B

Create Custom List or Table Styles

You have seen how to create styles for text and paragraphs. In this topic, you will create styles for lists and tables. Creating your own custom styles for the text in your document can save you time when you need to use the style again. You can create styles for other elements in Word documents, including lists and tables. The formatting options are directly related to the element for which you're creating a style, so the options for creating lists and tables will be different from what was available for text and paragraphs.

List Styles

You can create and modify list and table styles using the **Create New Style from Formatting** dialog box. The bullet characteristics and table border options are available for the list and table styles, respectively. Selecting a list prior to opening the dialog box enables you to see the existing list formats. Selecting a formatted table does not show the existing format, and you need to manually format the style for the table.

For lists, you can also use the **Define New List Style** dialog box. You open this dialog box from the **Multilevel List** gallery on the **Home** tab in the **Paragraph** group.

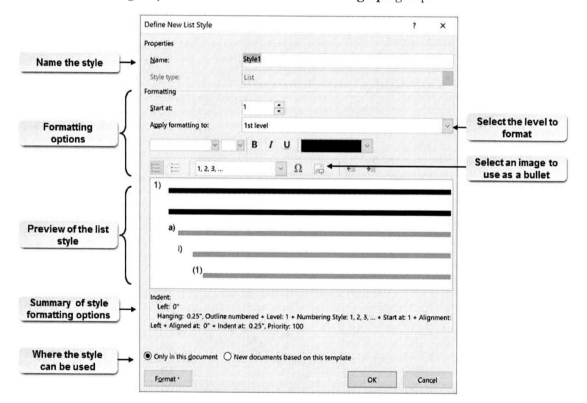

Figure 2-11: In the Define New List Style dialog box, you can configure how Word formats each level of the list.

Table Styles

When you create a new table style, you can specify the style Word uses for each of the components in the table, including the whole table, the header row, even rows, odd rows, and other table components.

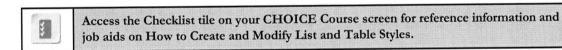

Figure 2-12: In the Create New Style from Formatting dialog box, you can specify how Word formats each table component.

Access the Checklist tile on your CHOICE Course screen for reference information and job aids on How to Create and Modify List and Table Styles.

ACTIVITY 2-2
Creating and Modifying List and Table Styles

Before You Begin

My New store flyer.docx is open.

Scenario

The director of Building with Heart would like you to format the bulleted list in the flyer to stand out. She saw another store's advertisement where they used a graphic for the bullets, and she would like you to find something that would work for the HouSalvage store. She would also like the table with store locations and hours to look more professional, rather than just rows and columns of information. To save time when the second new store opens in a month, you decide to create list and table styles for the list and table in the document.

1. Select the bulleted list and create a new list style.
   a) At the bottom of page one, select the bulleted list in the document and change the font size to 14.

   b) On the **Home** tab, in the **Paragraph** group, select the **Multilevel List** button.
   c) Select **Define New List Style**. The **Define New List Style** dialog box opens.
   d) In the **Name** text box, type *Sale categories*

   e) Select the **Picture** icon.
   f) In the **Bing Image Search** text box, type *hammer* and then select the **Search** icon.

   g) Close the message stating that images in the search results might be subject to copyright.
   h) Select a hammer from the results of your search.
   i) Select **Insert**. Word displays the hammer as the icon for the first item in the list.

   j) In the **Formatting** section, from the **Apply formatting to** drop-down list, select **2nd level**.
   k) Select the **Picture** icon.
   l) Search for **wrench** and select a wrench from the results.
   m) Select **Insert**.
   n) Near the bottom of the dialog box, select **New documents based on this template**. Selecting this option enables you to use this list style in new documents that you create, because Word adds this list style to the Normal template.

o) Select **OK**. The bulleted list now uses hammers and wrenches instead of bullets for list items.

All plumbing supplies, including

Faucets

Pipes

2. Select the table and apply a built-in table style, then create a new table style with different settings.
   a) Select the table on the second page of the document.
   b) On the **Table Tools Design** tab, in the **Table Styles** group, select the **More** button.
   c) In the table styles gallery, select a red table style from the gallery to apply a built-in table style to the table. You are going to create a new table style based on the table style you select.

d) On the **Table Tools Design** tab, in the **Table Styles** group, select the **More** button again.
e) Select **New Table Style**. The **Create New Style from Formatting** dialog box is displayed.
f) In the **Name** text box, type *Store Location Table*

g) From the **Apply formatting to** drop-down list, select **Header row**.

Apply formatting to:	Header row
	Whole table
	Header row
	Total row
	First column
½ pt	Last column
	Odd banded rows
	Even banded rows
Jan	Odd banded columns
East 7	Even banded columns

h) From the **Fill Color** drop-down list, select a color for the header row.

i) From the **Apply formatting to** list, select **Even banded rows**.

j) From the **Fill Color** drop-down list, select a color to apply to the even rows of the table.

k) Select **New documents based on this template**.

l) Select **OK**.

3. Observe the new table style you created.

a) On the **Table Tools Design** tab, in the **Table Styles** group, select the **More** button to display the **Table Styles** gallery.

b) Under **Custom**, select **Store Location Table**, which is the style you just created.

Custom

Plain Store Location Table

4. Save and close the file.

TOPIC C

Apply Document Themes

You have seen how to use styles to apply the same formatting to document elements without the need to format them each time. Document themes enable you to create documents with consistent formatting. In this topic, you will apply document themes.

Remembering exactly which fonts, colors, and styles you used in a previous document can be difficult. Using themes, you can apply the same fonts, colors, and styles to any document quickly and easily.

Document Themes

A *document theme* is a THMX file that contains a set of theme colors, fonts, and effects such as lines and fill effects. It enables you to apply a consistent look to the fonts, colors, and graphic effects in your documents. Word contains built-in themes, and you can create your own theme by customizing an existing theme.

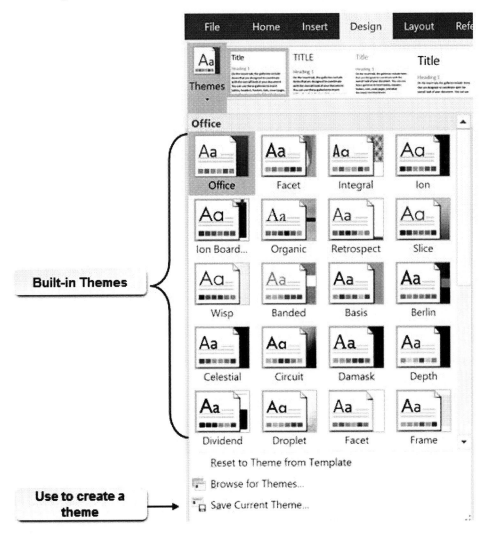

Figure 2-13: The Themes gallery includes preset themes that define the colors, fonts, and effects for a document.

Themes can also include **Page Background** settings. These settings can include the **Page Color** and **Page Border** settings. You probably don't want to apply a page color if you will be printing the document, because it uses a lot of toner or ink and the edges of the page will still be the color of the paper. If you need to print a single copy to show someone what color paper you want to use, that would work well. If you are going to use the document only in digital format, setting a page color should pose no problems.

Default Theme

The font scheme and color scheme in a theme are closely tied to the style sets. When you set the default theme, you also set the default style set.

The Themes Button

You use themes by selecting the **Design** tab and then, in the **Document Formatting** group, selecting **Themes**. Also in the **Document Formatting** group are the buttons for configuring theme colors, fonts, and effects.

Custom Themes

If none of the built-in themes meet your needs, you can create your own theme. Set the desired colors, fonts, and effects in your document and then save it as a new theme. By default, Word saves the theme in the Document Themes folder as the file type **Office Theme**. The Document Themes folder is located in the path **C:\Users*username*\AppData\Roaming\Microsoft\Templates \Document Themes**. By default, Windows 10 hides the C:\Users*username*\AppData folder, its contents, and all subfolders. You must save any custom themes you create to this folder if you want Word to display them in the **Themes** gallery.

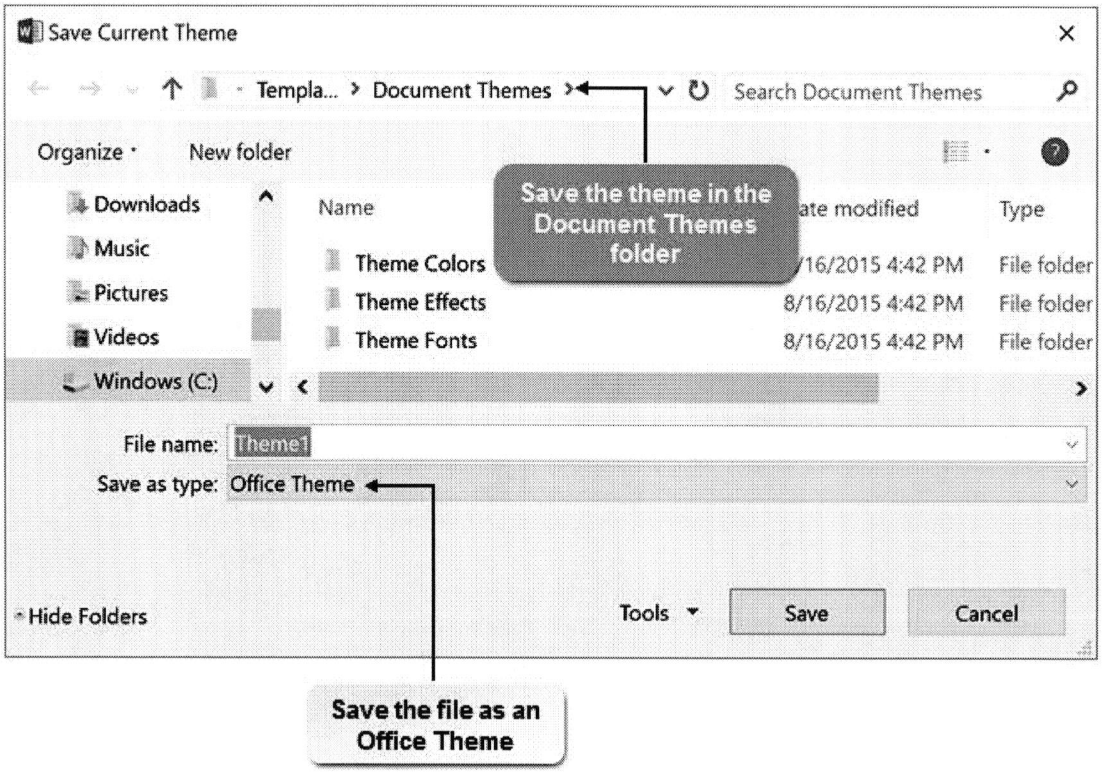

Figure 2-14: Word saves themes to the default Document Themes folder.

Share Custom Themes

If you want to share a custom theme you've created in Word, you can do so by copying the theme file from the **C:\Users***username***\AppData\Roaming\Microsoft\Templates\Document Themes** folder on your computer. Then, copy the theme file to the equivalent folder on another user's computer. Keep in mind that Windows hides these folders by default.

Custom Color Sets

In addition to support for creating custom themes (which include settings for colors, fonts, and effects), you can also create custom color and font sets. Use a custom color set to control all the colors Word uses for the various elements in your document. For example, you can set the dark and light colors for both the text and background; colors for all accents; and for a hyperlink. After you've chosen the colors you want to use, assign a name to the color set. Word displays the color set in the **Colors** drop-down list on the **Design** tab.

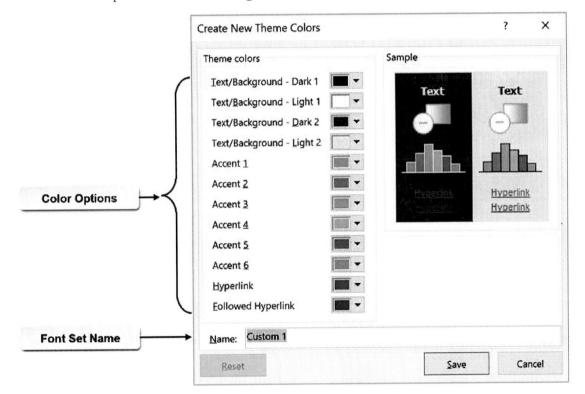

Figure 2–15: Custom color set

Sharing Custom Color Sets

When you create a custom color set, Word stores it in a file named ***filename*.xml**, where ***filename*** is the name you typed in the **Name** text box in the **Create New Theme Colors** dialog box. Word stores this file in the hidden folder **C:\Users***username***\AppData\Roaming\Microsoft \Templates\Theme Colors**. If you want to share a cusom color set, copy the color set file to the same folder on the user's computer with whom you want to share.

Custom Font Sets

Just as you can create a custom color set, so can you create a custom font set. The custom font set consists of a heading font and a body font, and a font set name. After you create the custom font set, Word displays the custom font set on the **Fonts** drop-down list on the **Design** tab.

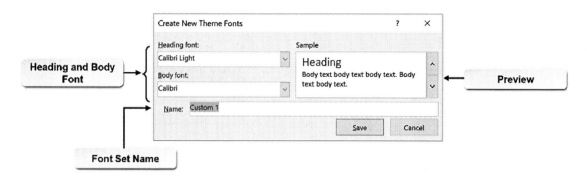

Figure 2-16: Custom font set

Sharing Custom Font Sets

When you create a custom font set, Word stores it in a file named *filename*.xml, where *filename* is the name you typed in the **Name** text box in the **Create New Theme Fonts** dialog box. Word stores this file in the hidden folder **C:\Users*username*\AppData\Roaming\Microsoft\Templates\Theme Fonts**. If you want to share a cusom font set, copy the font set file to the same folder on the user's computer with whom you want to share.

Guidelines for Formatting a Word Document

When you format a Word document, you can use a strategy that minimizes the number of steps required to format your document. To format a document effectively, use these guidelines:

- Apply a document theme first. When you apply a theme, you configure the colors, fonts, and graphic effects Word uses for your documents. For this reason, you want to select your document theme first. Otherwise, you will lose any individual changes you make to a document's formatting when you select a theme.
- If necessary, further customize your document by selecting text and applying changes such as the font style, color, or graphic effects.

> **Access the Checklist tile on your CHOICE Course screen for reference information and job aids on How to Apply Document Themes.**

ACTIVITY 2-3
Applying Document Themes

Data File

Desktop\Building with Heart\Customizing Formats Using Styles and Themes\HouSalvage Hiring.docx

Scenario

You are creating a document for Building with Heart's hiring initiative going on for the new store. You want to create a professional-looking document in a format that others can use again for additional documents in the future. You want to save the formatting in a way that makes it easy to use again.

 Note: You are going to format some of the document's elements so that you can see how selecting a theme overrides your changes.

1. Format some of the document's elements.
   a) From the **Desktop\Building with Heart\Customizing Formats Using Styles and Themes** folder, open **HouSalvage Hiring.docx**.
   b) Save the document as *My HouSalvage Hiring.docx*
   c) On the **Design** tab, in the **Page Background** group, select **Page Color**. Select a background color for the letter.
   d) On the **Design** tab, in the **Page Background** group, select **Page Borders**.
   e) In the **Borders and Shading** dialog box, below **Setting**, select **Box**.

Setting:

 <u>N</u>one

 Bo<u>x</u>

   f) From the **Color** drop-down list, select **Red**.
   g) In the **Apply to** drop-down list, verify that **Whole document** is selected and then select **OK**. You see a red border around the letter.

2. Apply a theme to your document.
   a) In the **Document Formatting** group, select **Themes**.
   b) Point to various themes and notice that the fonts, font sizes, and the page background color change as you preview the themes.
   c) Select a document theme. Notice that this theme changes the fonts but doesn't override the color you previously set for the page border. Word doesn't include the page background color in its themes.

3. Customize the theme.
   a) On the **Design** tab, in the **Document Formatting** group, select **Colors**.

      b) Point to various colors to see how the document colors change.

      c) Select a different color scheme.

      d) On the **Design** tab, in the **Document Formatting** group, select **Fonts**, and then select a font other than Calibri.

4. Save the current theme.

      a) On the **Design** tab, in the **Document Formatting** group, select **Themes**.

      b) Select **Save Current Theme**.

      c) Save the theme as *My Hiring Theme*

5. Observe your new theme in the **Themes** gallery.

      a) Select **Design→Document Formatting→Themes**. Verify that under **Themes**, the **Custom** gallery shows **My Hiring Theme**.

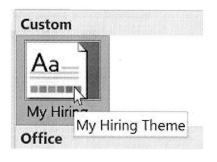

      b) Save the file and close Word.

Summary

In this lesson, you created customized styles and themes. First, you customized character, paragraph, and linked styles for text. Then, you customized list and table styles. Finally, you customized document themes. These customizations help you ensure that you apply the same formatting to any documents to which you apply the themes and styles.

Does your organization currently use customized styles and themes? If so, are there any changes you would make to them? If not, what style and theme features would you add to your custom styles and themes?

Why do you think styles and themes might be important to an organization?

> **Note:** Check your CHOICE Course screen for opportunities to interact with your classmates, peers, and the larger CHOICE online community about the topics covered in this course or other topics you are interested in. From the Course screen you can also access available resources for a more continuous learning experience.

3 Inserting Content Using Quick Parts

Lesson Time: 45 minutes

Lesson Objectives

In this lesson, you will insert content using quick parts. You will:

- Insert building blocks into a document.

- Create and modify building blocks.

- Insert fields for variable content into documents.

Lesson Introduction

You have inserted many types of elements in your Microsoft® Word documents such as tables, text boxes, and images. In this lesson, through the use of Quick Parts, you will see how you can easily add default and custom content to your documents. Using Quick Parts provides access to the default Word galleries and allows you to save content to the **Quick Parts** list.

TOPIC A

Insert Building Blocks

You probably have some organizational content that should be formatted and worded the same between documents. Rather than having to type and format or copy the content each time you need to use it, you can create blocks of content to reuse for each document.

Quick Parts

You use the **Quick Parts** button on the **Insert** tab to insert reusable pieces of content in your documents. The **Quick Parts** gallery includes built-in building blocks, building blocks you saved to the gallery, AutoText entries, document properties, and fields.

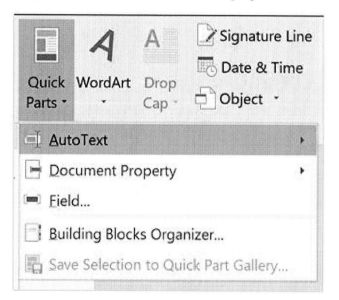

Figure 3-1: The Quick Parts menu.

The following table describes the **Quick Parts** menu options.

Quick Parts Option	Description
AutoText	Enables you to store content and then reuse it in any document. From this menu, you can insert AutoText that has already been saved and save selected content to the **AutoText** menu.
Document Property	Enables you to insert document properties. You can view or change the document properties. From the **File** tab, select **Info** to view the document properties. To change properties, hover over the property and then enter the information.
Field	Enables you to insert a placeholder for data that might change. For example, inserting the fields **Page** and **PageRef** with the word "of" in between would give you "1 of 10" if you were on the first page of a 10-page document and "5 of 10" if you were on the fifth page of a 10-page document.

Quick Parts Option	Description
Building Blocks Organizer	Displays the **Building Blocks Organizer** dialog box. From there, you can view the available building blocks, preview them, edit their properties, and save and delete building blocks.

 Note: If you have a word that you consistently misspell, you can add the incorrect spelling to an AutoText entry, and configure it to change to the correct spelling. If your company is known by a short name and you need to type the long name, you can use an AutoText entry to convert the short name to the long name.

Building Blocks

A *building block* is content that has been formatted and stored for use in any Word document. Word includes built-in building blocks, and you can also create your own building blocks. A building block can contain any type of information, including headers, footers, graphics, and text all formatted to your specifications.

Word stores building blocks in a number of galleries, categories, and templates. Galleries include **AutoText**, **Bibliography**, **Cover Pages**, **Page Numbers**, **Text Boxes**, **Watermarks**, and more.

The Building Blocks Organizer Dialog Box

Any content that you can select in a Word document you can save as a building block. Each building block is a reusable block of content. There are many built-in building blocks in Word. Through the **Building Blocks Organizer** dialog box, you can insert, organize, and modify the building blocks.

The right pane of the **Building Blocks Organizer** dialog box shows a preview of the block you select in the center pane of the dialog box. You can sort the dialog box content using the headers in the left pane.

You can edit the properties of a building block, delete a building block, or insert a building block into your document.

Figure 3-2: The Building Blocks Organizer dialog box.

The Building Blocks Pane

The **Building Blocks** pane of the **Building Blocks Organizer** dialog box lists all available building blocks. Each building block lists several details.

Building Blocks Pane	Description
Name	A unique name for the building block.
Gallery	The gallery in which Word lists the building block. Galleries throughout Word include items shown in the **Building Blocks Organizer** dialog box.
Category	The category within the gallery where Word lists the building block. For example, the **Page Number** gallery has a category named **With Shapes**.
Template	The template in which Word stores the building block. By default, Word stores the built-in building blocks in **Built-in Building Blocks.dotx**. When you create your own building blocks, by default, Word stores them in **Normal.dotx**.
Behavior	What is inserted: • Insert content only. • Insert content in its own page. • Insert content in its own paragraph.
Description	A short description of the building block.

 Access the Checklist tile on your CHOICE Course screen for reference information and job aids on How to Insert Building Blocks.

ACTIVITY 3-1
Inserting Building Blocks

Data File

Desktop\Building with Heart\Inserting Content Using Quick Parts\Training Manual.docx

Scenario

You have been gathering information for a training manual to train the employees that are being hired for the new HouSalvage stores. You have the basic information, but want to make it look more like a professional manual with headers, footers, and a table of contents. The **Title** property for the file has been set to **Training Manual**.

1. Open the **Training Manual.docx** file.
   a) From the **Desktop\Building with Heart\Inserting Content Using Quick Parts** folder, open **Training Manual.docx**.
   b) Save the document as *My Training Manual.docx*

2. Use the **Building Blocks Organizer** dialog box to insert a table of contents.
   a) If paragraph marks are not enabled, on the **Home** tab, in the **Paragraph** group, select **Show/Hide ¶**.
   b) Scroll through the document to see what is in the file.
   c) Position the cursor just before the page break on the first page.
   d) On the **Insert** tab, in the **Text** group, select **Quick Parts**.

Quick Parts ▾

   e) Select **Building Blocks Organizer**.
   f) Select **Name** to sort the list in order by name.
   g) Scroll down and select the **Automatic Table 2** building block.

 Note: You can expand the column headings to view more of the information and names in the columns. Drag the separator between the column headings to expand the width of the column.

   h) Select **Insert**. Word uses all of the text formatted as **Heading 1**, **Heading 2**, and so on to create the table of contents automatically.

 Note: If you see the field codes instead of the field results, press **Alt+F9** to toggle field codes off.

3. Add the **Sideline Headers** building block.
   a) Position the cursor on the second page of the document.
   b) On the **Insert** tab, in the **Text** group, select **Quick Parts**.
   c) Select **Building Blocks Organizer**.

d) Scroll down and select the **Sideline Headers** building block. You can type *S* to skip to the first building block that has a name that begins with the letter "S."

> **Note:** Word displays "Sideline" in the **Name** column and "Headers" in the **Gallery** column.

Building Blocks Organizer ? ✕

Building blocks:

Name	Gallery	Cat...	Tem...	Beh...	Des
Semaphor...	Text Boxes	Buil...	Buil...	Inse...	Pull
Semaphor...	Text Boxes	Buil...	Buil...	Inse...	Side
Sideline	Footers	Buil...	Buil...	Inse...	Pag
Sideline	Headers	Buil...	Buil...	Inse...	Doc
Sideline	Cover Pa...	Buil...	Buil...	Inse...	Cer
Sideline Q...	Text Boxes	Buil...	Buil...	Inse...	Left
Sideline Si...	Text Boxes	Buil...	Buil...	Inse...	Side
Simple Q...	Text Boxes	Buil...	Buil...	Inse...	Sha

Click a building block to see its preview

Sideline
Document title with vertical accent bar

Edit Properties... **Delete** **Insert**

Close

e) Select **Insert**. Word inserts a header and uses the **Title** property that was already defined for this document.

f) On the **Header & Footer Tools Design** tab, check the **Different First Page** check box to prevent the header from displaying on the first page of the training manual.

4. Add the **Sideline Footers** building block.

   a) Select **Insert→Text→Quick Parts**.
   b) Select **Building Blocks Organizer**.
   c) Scroll down and select the **Sideline Footers** building block.
   d) Select **Insert**. Word inserts a footer that displays the page number at the bottom of every page except the first page. This is because you have already checked the **Different First Page** check box.
   e) Double-click in the body of the document to close the header and footer panes.
   f) Turn off the display of paragraph marks.
   g) Scroll through the document and verify that **Training Manual** appears at the top of every page except for the cover page, and that the footer contains page numbers starting after the cover page.

5. Save the document.

TOPIC B

Create and Modify Building Blocks

You have seen how easily you can use built-in Quick Parts to format your document. If you frequently use the same text with the same formatting and copy the information from one document to another to make sure that you use consistent wording and formatting, you can create your own building blocks to make custom reusable content. In this topic, you will create your own building blocks.

The Create New Building Block Dialog Box

You can create and select content that you want to make reusable. Configure the Quick Part through the **Create New Building Block** dialog box to specify a name, gallery, category, description, and in which template you want to store the building block. By default, Word stores new quick parts or building blocks in the template named **Building Blocks.dotx**. Saving to this template makes the building blocks available to every document you create. When you specify a gallery, the building block will appear in that gallery elsewhere in Word as well as in the **Building Blocks Organizer** dialog box. The category you specify adds the item to the gallery for the selected category.

When you create a new building block, you can specify for Word to insert the content you specify as content only, content in a new page, or content in a new paragraph. Use the **Insert content only** option if you want to insert the content of the building block at the current location of your cursor. Choose the **Content in a new page** option if you want to insert the building block's content on a separate page. Finally, choose the **Content in a new paragraph** option if you know you want to insert the building block's content on the same page as your cursor but in a separate paragraph.

Create New Building Block	? ✕
Name:	HouSalvage Name and Tagline
Gallery:	Quick Parts
Category:	General
Description:	Use this building block to insert the HouSalvage store name and tagline.
Save in:	Building Blocks
Options:	Insert content only
	OK Cancel

Figure 3-3: The Create New Building Block dialog box.

Sharing Building Blocks with Other Users

If you want to share the quick parts or building blocks you've created in Word with other users, you can do so by copying the **Building Blocks.dotx** template from the appropriate folder on your computer and placing it in the equivalent folder on other users' computers. By default, Word 2016 stores the **Building Blocks.dotx** template in the hidden folder **C:\Users*username*\AppData \Roaming\Microsoft\Document Building Blocks\1033\16**. After you've copied the **Building Blocks.dotx** template, store the copy in the same hidden folder for the user with which you want to share the template.

 Note: To view hidden folders in **File Explorer**, on the **View** tab, in the **Show/hide** group, select the **Hidden items** check box.

Building Block Modification Options

Through the **Modify Building Block** dialog box, you can modify the content of both custom and built-in building blocks. Modifying a building block overwrites the original building block content. You can modify the properties of the building block, including the name, gallery, category, and description.

If you need to modify the content, insert the building block into a document. Make the required changes. Save the building block with the same name as the original building block. You will be prompted to decide whether or not you want to redefine the building block.

 Access the Checklist tile on your CHOICE Course screen for reference information and job aids on How to Create a New Building Block.

 Access the Checklist tile on your CHOICE Course screen for reference information and job aids on How to Modify an Existing Building Block.

ACTIVITY 3-2
Creating and Modifying Building Blocks

Before You Begin
My Training Manual.docx is open.

Scenario
The training manual includes a page of components that you frequently use when creating store flyers. The manual says you can copy the components when you need them. Now that you know about building blocks, you want to create building blocks from these components.

1. Create building blocks from the title and subtitle in the document, and the star graphic.
   a) Scroll to the top of page 4 where you see the heading "Creating the Monthly Sales Flyer."
   b) Select the **HouSalvage Recycling Centers** name and tagline shown in red type.
   c) On the **Insert** tab, in the **Text** group, select **Quick Parts**.
   d) Select **Save Selection to Quick Part Gallery**. The **Create New Building Block** dialog box is displayed.
   e) Configure these settings for the new building block:

Create New Building Block	? ✕
Name:	HouSalvage Name and Tagline
Gallery:	Quick Parts
Category:	General
Description:	This building block inserts the HouSalvage store name and tagline.
Save in:	Building Blocks.dotx
Options:	Insert content in its own page
	OK Cancel

   f) Select **OK**.

2. Create a building block to insert the star graphic on page 5 of the document.
   a) On page 5, select the star graphic. The graphic needs to have a solid blue line around it rather than the dotted blue line. If the dotted line is displayed, click it and it should become a solid line.

b) Configure these settings for the new building block:

Create New Building Block	? ✕
Name:	Discount Star
Gallery:	Quick Parts ⌄
Category:	General ⌄
Description:	Inserts the red discount star into the document.
Save in:	Building Blocks.dotx ⌄
Options:	Insert content only ⌄
	OK Cancel

3. Modify the **Discount Star** building block to change the content to 25% off.
   a) On page 5, select the star graphic.
   b) Change the **15** to *25*
   c) If necessary, scroll down. Select the star graphic again.
   d) On the **Insert** tab, in the **Text** group, select **Quick Parts**.
   e) Select **Save Selection to Quick Part Gallery**. The **Create New Building Block** dialog box is displayed.
   f) In the **Name** box, type *Discount Star* as the name for the building block.
   g) Select **OK**.
   h) Select **Yes** to verify that you want to redefine the building block.

4. Rename the **Discount Star** building block to **Discount Star 25**.
   a) On the **Insert** tab, in the **Text** group, select **Quick Parts**.
   b) Select **Building Blocks Organizer**.
   c) Select the **Discount Star** building block.

   > **Note:** If necessary, select the **Name** column to sort the list of building blocks.

   d) Select **Edit Properties**.
   e) In the **Name** box, modify the name to be *Discount Star 25*
   f) Select **OK**.
   g) Select **Yes**.
   h) Select **Close**.

5. Verify that Word displays the **Discount Star 25** graphic on the **Quick Parts** menu.
   a) Open the **Quick Parts** menu to verify that the **Discount Star 25** graphic is listed, and then close the menu.
   b) Save and close the file.

6. Insert the custom building blocks you just created into a new document.
   a) Select the **File** tab and then select **New**.
   b) In the list of templates, select **Blank document**.
   c) Select the **Insert** tab.

d) In the **Text** group, select **Quick Parts**.

e) In the list of building blocks, select **HouSalvage Name and Tagline**. Word inserts the HouSalvage store name and its tagline into your document. Notice that the content includes the formatting in addition to the text.

f) From the **Quick Parts** list, select the **Discount Star** building block to insert the discount star with 15% off.

g) Close the new document without saving your changes.

TOPIC C

Insert Fields Using Quick Parts

You have used built-in Quick Parts and created your own building blocks to add to the **Quick Parts** menu. The **Quick Parts** menu also includes the ability to insert fields for variable content in your document. In this topic, you will add fields to your document.

If you have content that is regularly updated, you can use fields to hold that data. Whenever you need to change the data, you can just update the fields.

Fields

A *field* is a placeholder that displays variable data. Examples of fields that are automatically inserted with some Word commands include the date, time, document properties, and page numbers. You can also insert fields manually to include variable information in a mail merge, such as customer names and addresses. Fields can also be used to perform calculations.

A field works because there is programming contained in *field codes*. Field code programming processes the command identified in the field code and displays the result in the document as a field value. The result is displayed by default, but you can display the field code instead. Press **Alt+F9** to toggle between showing field codes and field results. The value in the field changes as data or conditions change; the field code does not change.

Field Codes	Field Code Values
{ DATE \@ "M/d/yy" * MERGEFORMAT }	9/8/2016
{ DATE \@ "dddd, MMMM d, yyyy" * MERGEFORMAT }	Tuesday, September 8, 2016
{ PAGE * Arabic * MERGEFORMAT }	1
{ AUTHOR * MERGEFORMAT }	Jane Learner
{ USERNAME * MERGEFORMAT }	Jane Learner
{ AUTONUM * Arabic }	1
{ LISTNUM }	1)

Figure 3–4: Examples of field codes and the field results.

Field Code Syntax

A field code is contained between curly braces. The field name is the first element inside the braces. Most field codes include properties, which make up the second element. If the property contains spaces, Word encloses the property in quotes. Optional switches, if available for a field, are the third element.

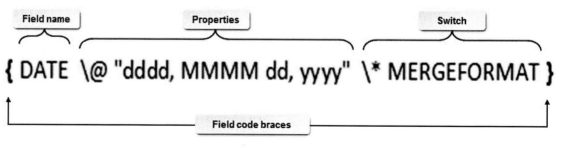

Figure 3–5: Field code syntax.

In the previous figure, the field code will insert the date. The properties specify the format in which the date will be displayed. For example, Saturday, December 31, 2016. The switch in the figure is used to retain the formatting of the field when the field is updated.

The Field Dialog Box

You can manually insert fields into a document, but it is much easier to insert them through the **Field** dialog box. The syntax is automatically configured for you as you build your field code in the dialog box.

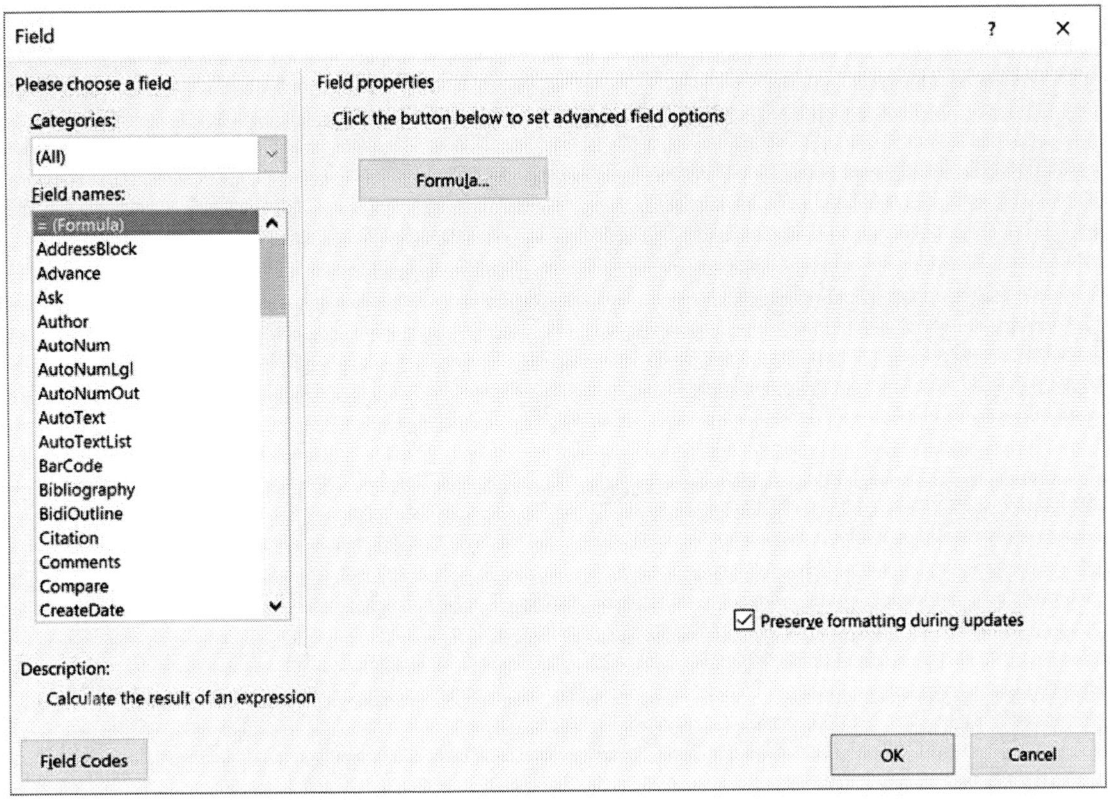

Figure 3-6: The center and right panes of the Field dialog box change depending on which field name you select in the left pane.

The **Field Codes** button shows or hides the field codes in the dialog box. If field codes are displayed, the dialog box looks like the following figure.

Figure 3–7: You can show the field codes in the Field dialog box.

Field Codes

The list of field codes that you can use in Word is found in the **Field Code** dialog box. By default, all of the field codes in all categories are listed.

Field Categories

If you want to show only the field codes related to a particular category, you can change the **Categories** list in the **Field** dialog box to show one of the following field categories:

- **Date and Time**
- **Document Automation**
- **Document Information**
- **Equations and Formulas**
- **Index and Tables**
- **Links and References**
- **Mail Merge**
- **Numbering**
- **User Information**

> Access the Checklist tile on your CHOICE Course screen for reference information and job aids on **How to Insert Fields Using Quick Parts.**

ACTIVITY 3–3
Inserting Fields Using Quick Parts

Data File

Desktop\Building with Heart\Inserting Content Using Quick Parts\HouSalvage Schedule.docx

Scenario

You have a schedule of when employees work. You would like to add the date it was printed and a title in the header. You would also like the page numbers in the format "Page x of y" and the file name to appear in the footer.

1. Open the **HouSalvage Schedule** document.
   a) From the **Desktop\Building with Heart\Inserting Content Using Quick Parts** folder, open **HouSalvage Schedule.docx**.
   b) Save the document as *My HouSalvage Schedule.docx*

2. Create a header that displays the document title.
   a) Double-click at the top of the document in the whitespace to open the **Header** area. If you double-clicked the title **HouSalvage Recycling Centers Schedule**, click in the whitespace of the header to deselect the title.
   b) On the **Insert** tab, in the **Text** group, select **Quick Parts**.
   c) Select **Field**.
   d) In the **Please choose a field** section, from the **Categories** drop-down list, select **Document Information**.
   e) From the **Field names** list, select **Title**. The **Title** is a document property that was previously set for this document.
   f) Select **OK**.

3. Modify the header to include the date the document was last saved.
   a) In the **Header** area, press **Tab** twice to position the next field so that it's right aligned.
   b) Type *Last Saved:*
   c) From the **Quick Parts** menu, select **Field**.
   d) From the **Categories** drop-down list, select **Date and Time**.
   e) From the **Field names** list, select **SaveDate**.
   f) In the **Date formats** section, select the date with the format **M/d/yyyy**. The selection will show today's date.

   > **Caution:** Even if the date format looks like it's already selected, you need to manually select it.

   g) Select **OK**.
   h) Observe the date shown in the header.

4. View the field codes.
   a) Press **Alt+F9**.
   b) Observe that Word now displays the field codes instead of the field results.
   c) Press **Alt+F9** to turn field codes off.

5. Create a footer with page numbers and the file name with the path.
   a) Scroll to the **Footer** area at the bottom of the page.

b) From the **Quick Parts** menu, select **Field**.

c) From the **Categories** list, select **Numbering**.

d) From the **Field names** list, select **Page**, and then select **OK**.

e) After the **Page** field, press the **Spacebar**, type *of*, and then press the **Spacebar**.

f) From the **Quick Parts** menu, select **Field**.

g) From the **Categories** list, select **Document Information**.

h) From the **Field names** list, select **NumPages**, and then select **OK**.

i) Press **Enter**.

j) From the **Quick Parts** menu, select **Field**.

k) From the **Field names** list, select **FileName**.

l) In the **Field options** section, check the **Add path to filename** check box.

m) Select **OK**. Observe the path and file name in the footer.

n) Save the file and close Word.

Summary

In this lesson, you used Quick Parts to add a variety of content to your documents. First, you inserted built-in building blocks. Then, you created and modified your own building blocks. Finally, you inserted fields in your document. From the **Quick Parts** menu, you can manage and use reusable content, providing quick access to the content in a central location. Now that you have added various types of content to your document, you are ready to create full document templates.

How might you use building blocks in your documents?

When might you use field codes in your documents?

 Note: Check your CHOICE Course screen for opportunities to interact with your classmates, peers, and the larger CHOICE online community about the topics covered in this course or other topics you are interested in. From the Course screen you can also access available resources for a more continuous learning experience.

4 Using Templates to Automate Document Formatting

Lesson Time: 30 minutes

Lesson Objectives

In this lesson, you will use templates to automate document formatting. You will:

- Create a document using a template.

- Create a custom template.

- Manage templates with the Building Blocks Organizer.

Lesson Introduction

You have seen how using styles and Quick Parts can give your documents a consistent look and feel. Using those components can also save you time when formatting your documents. In this lesson, you will create templates, which also help you create a consistent look for your documents.

TOPIC A

Create a Document Using a Template

When you create a document, you often need to set up the page layout, determine which styles to use, and set up how the document is formatted. If you have documents that use the same page layout and styles, and even some of the same content, you can save time if you base your document on a template. In this topic, you will create a document using a template.

Templates in Word

A *template* is a special type of Microsoft® Word document containing the desired formatting that you can use as the starting point for creating new Word documents. When you create any Word document, Word bases that document on a template. A template contains the layout, formatting, and (possibly) text that you want to use in any document based on that template. Using a template creates a copy of it as a Word DOCX file so that the existing content in the template file is not overwritten. Word documents have the .docx extension; in contrast, template files have the .dotx extension. If the template file contains macros, Word uses the extension .dotm for the template.

Word attaches templates to a document. The attached template provides access to the styles, macros, and other items defined in the template. You can change which template Word attaches to your document, which gives you access to the styles, macros, and other items defined in that template, without losing the content in your current document. By default, Word attaches the Normal template to your documents if you don't specify a different template.

 Note: Macros are covered in the *Microsoft® Office Word 2016: Part 3* course.

Types of Templates

Word includes two types of templates. You use document templates to create documents with specific custom formatting. In contrast, Word uses the Normal template for toolbars and formatting that apply to all open documents. If a document template and the Normal template contain styles that have the same name, the document settings override the Normal template settings. When you create a new document, if you don't use a template, Word uses the settings in the default template, Normal.dotm. In addition, Word applies any changes you make to Normal.dotm to all documents.

New

Search for online templates 🔍

Suggested searches: Business Personal Industry Print Design Sets Education Event

Blank do...   Welco...   Single...   Blog p...   Bande...

Cover l...   Spring...   Person...   Busine...   Sales i...

Figure 4-1: There are many templates available online.

Fields and Forms

Some templates include fields, forms, or both to make it easier for you to add data to your document. The fields are placeholders in the document that indicate what type of content you should add to a specific location within the document. Forms might have controls such as drop-down lists or placeholder text you can replace with a single click.

 Note: To learn more about forms and form controls in templates, search "forms and form controls" in the **Tell me what you want to do** text box.

Template Categories

Word includes a great number of templates you can use, and you can find even more templates for Word online. When you select **File→New**, you can select one of the templates displayed in the **New** pane of **Backstage** view or search online templates. When you search online, Word displays thumbnails of templates along with a **Category** list you can use to help you narrow down your search.

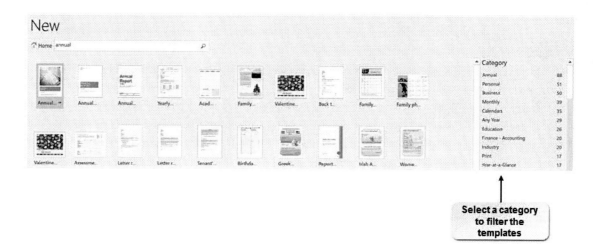

Figure 4-2: You can filter your template search by Category.

Template Storage Locations

Word saves the templates you create or modify in the **User templates** default folder. Word also saves the Normal.dotm global template there. Advertised templates are the templates included with Word. If you select a template that Word has not already installed, you will be prompted to install it. If your network administrator has created a shared location for templates, those are stored in the network directory the administrator set up.

The following table lists the locations where Word stores templates.

Template Type	Stored In
Advertised and installed templates	\Program Files (x86)\Microsoft Office\root\templates*Language ID Number* (for 32-bit Office 2016) or \Program Files\Microsoft Office\root\templates*Language ID Number* (for 64-bit Office 2016)
User templates	\Users*username*\Documents\Custom Office Templates
Workgroup templates	A shared network location

 Note: The Language ID for English (US) is 1033, and for German it is 1031. You can find other language IDs at **http://support.microsoft.com/kb/221435**.

Access the Checklist tile on your CHOICE Course screen for reference information and job aids on How to Create a Document Using a Template.

ACTIVITY 4–1
Creating a Document Using a Template

Scenario

It is the week before the grand opening of the new HouSalvage Recycling Center and you want to write a letter to your new neighbors inviting them to a special preview night before the grand opening. It has been a long week, so instead of coming up with a format for the letter, you want to use one of the templates included with Word.

1. Create a new document based on a template.
   a) In **Word**, select **File→New**.
   b) In the **Search for online templates** text box, type *Letters* and then press **Enter**.
   c) In the **Category** pane, select **Business**.
   d) Select **Letterhead (Red and Black design)**. (This is typically the second template displayed.) A dialog box opens with a preview of the template and a brief description.

Letterhead (Red and Black design)

Provided by: Microsoft Corporation

Use this bold, graphic letterhead template for your business. Personalize it with your company logo and change the colors using built-in themes. Part of the Red and Black design set.

Download size: 91 KB

Create

   e) Press the **Right Arrow** key. You can browse through the available templates with descriptions using the left and right arrows.
   f) Press the **Left Arrow** key to display the **Letterhead (Red and Black design)** template.
   g) Select **Create**.

2. Edit the content of the document.
   a) Select **Date**.

b) From the **Publish Date** drop-down list, select today's date.

c) Click in the **Name and Address** placeholder.
d) Type *Frank Stevens* and press **Enter**.
e) Type an address of your choosing.
f) Select **Recipient** and then type *Frank*
g) Observe the structure of the rest of the letter. You can click in the paragraphs to replace the body of the letter. At the bottom of the letter, the template has additional fields where you could type the company information and add a logo.

[Company]

Tel [Telephone]   [Address]   [Website]   replace with
Fax [Fax]   [City, ST ZIP]   [Email]   LOGO

h) Save the document in the folder **Desktop\Building with Heart\Using Templates to Automate Document Formatting** as *My HouSalvage Letter* and close it.

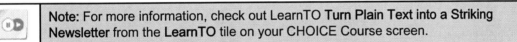

Figure 4-3: Word template and a document created from the template.

3. Close the document.

> **Note:** For more information, check out LearnTO **Turn Plain Text into a Striking Newsletter** from the **LearnTO** tile on your CHOICE Course screen.

TOPIC B

Create and Modify a Template

You have seen how useful a template can be to create documents with a consistent look, with formatting already applied, and in some cases, with content already in the document. There might be times when the templates that are available don't quite meet your needs. You can modify existing templates or create new templates, which is what you will do in this topic.

Template Creation Options

You can create templates from an existing document or from another template. To save a document as a template, specify the **Save as type** as **Word Template**. By default, Word stores custom templates in the folder **C:\Users*username*\Documents\Custom Office Templates**. To create a template from an existing template, open it from the templates list in **Backstage** view, make the desired changes, and save it again as a Word template with a new name.

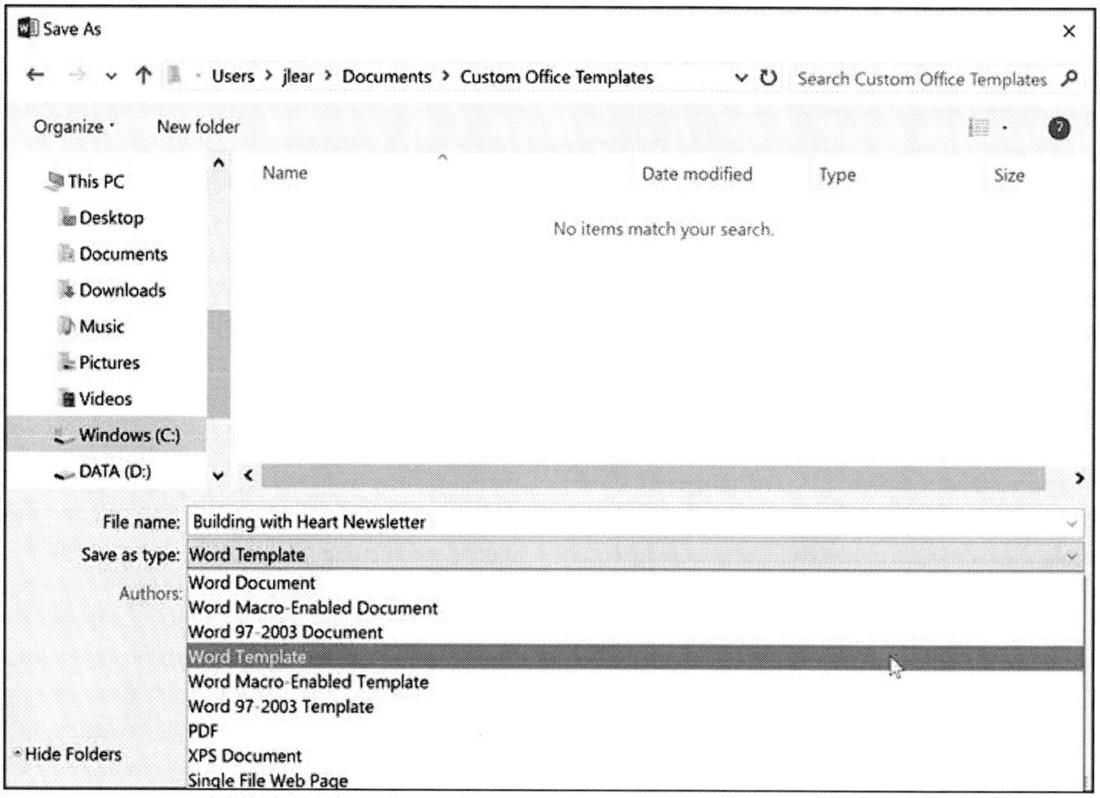

Figure 4–4: Saving a file as a template.

MacroButton Fields

You include the **MacroButton** field in a template to provide a single-click placeholder for text. You can also use the **MacroButton** field to run a macro that prompts the user for input. To use it just as a placeholder, use the **NoMacro** argument with the **MacroButton** field name.

Syntax:

{ MacroButton NoMacro DisplayTextInstruction }

Example:
{ MacroButton NoMacro (Type Text Here) }

After turning off Field Code Display, you will see:
(Type Text Here)

Figure 4–5: The syntax for adding placeholder text with instructions.

Note: To insert the braces in the document, press **Ctrl+F9**; you cannot just type {}.

The Default Template Location

You might want Word to store the templates you create in a different location than the default location. Some users prefer to have the templates in the same location. If you prefer to have them in a separate location, you can specify the location in the **Word Options** dialog box.

Access the Checklist tile on your CHOICE Course screen for reference information and job aids on How to Create a Template.

ACTIVITY 4-2
Creating a Template

Data File

Desktop\Building with Heart\Using Templates to Automate Document Formatting\Training Manual.docx

Scenario

You like the style that you used to create the HouSalvage Recycling Centers training manual. You want to save elements of this document to a template so that you can create future HouSalvage documents in the same style.

---

1. Delete content from the document.
    a) From the **Desktop\Building with Heart\Using Templates to Automate Document Formatting** folder, open the **Training Manual** document.
    b) You want to keep the red page border, Building with Heart logo, and the HouSalvage Recycling Centers name and tagline in the template. Delete the other elements of the document.

2. Add a text placeholder for the document content.
    a) Move your cursor to a new line below the HouSalvage Recycling Centers line and tagline. Verify that the text style is **Normal**.
    b) Press **Ctrl+F9** to insert field code braces.
    c) Between the braces, type *MacroButton NoMacro [Type the document content here]* to add a placeholder with instructions to the template.

{ MacroButton NoMacro [Type the document content here] }

3. Save the file as *My HouSalvage Template* in the **Custom Office Templates** folder.
    a) On the **Quick Access Toolbar**, select **Save As**.
    b) From the **Save as type** drop-down list, select **Word Template (*.dotx)**. Word changes to the **C:\Users*user_name*\Documents\Custom Office Templates** folder.
    c) In the **File name** text box, type *My HouSalvage Template* and then select **Save**.
    d) Close the document.

4. Use **My HouSalvage Template** to create a new document.
    a) In Word, select **File→New**.

b) Below the **Search for online templates** text box, select **PERSONAL**.

c) Select **My HouSalvage Template**. Word creates a new document from the template you saved.
d) Select the **Type the document content here** MacroButton placeholder. Type some content and observe that the placeholder works properly.
e) Close the document without saving.

Template Modification

After you have created a template, you might find you need to make changes to it. Modifying a template enables you to make changes that will be available in all new documents you create from the template. Keep in mind that when you want to open a template to make changes to it, Word stores template files in the folder **C:\Users***username***\Documents\Custom Office Templates**. You will need to open this folder when you want to modify a template.

 Access the Checklist tile on your **CHOICE** Course screen for reference information and job aids on **How to Modify a Template**.

ACTIVITY 4–3
Modifying a Template

Before You Begin

You have created a custom template named **My HouSalvage Template.dotx** and stored it in the **Custom Office Templates** folder within your **Documents** folder.

Scenario

You have found that you frequently add the date to documents you create based on the **My HouSalvage Template.dotx** template. You would like to add the date to this template so that any new documents you create based on the template will include the date.

1. Open the template **My HouSalvage Template.dotx**.
   a) Select **File** and then select **Browse**.
   b) If necessary, browse to select the folder **C:\Users\username\Documents\Custom Office Templates**.
   c) From the drop-down list next to the **File name** text box, if necessary, select **Word Templates (*.dotx)**.
   d) In the file list, select **My HouSalvage Template.dotx** and select **Open**.

2. Add the current date to the template.
   a) Press **Alt+F9** to display the field code you added as a placeholder for text.
   b) Place your cursor after the field code and press **Enter** to start a new line.
   c) Press **Alt+F9** to hide the field code.
   d) On the **Insert** tab, in the **Text** group, select **Date & Time**.
   e) In the **Available formats** list, select the date format you want to use.
   f) Select the **Update automatically** check box and then select **OK**.
   g) Save the template with the same filename.
   h) Close the template.

3. Verify that the template includes the current date in new documents you create.
   a) Select **File→New**.
   b) Below the **Search for online templates** text box, select **PERSONAL**.
   c) Select **My HouSalvage Template**. Verify that your new document has the current date below the tagline.
   d) Select the **Type the document content here** MacroButton placeholder. Type some content and observe that the placeholder works properly.
   e) Close the document without saving.

TOPIC C

Manage Templates with the Template Organizer

You have seen how you can create custom templates to simplify the process of creating new documents with specific styles and other settings. But what if you have some styles or macros in a custom template that you want to make available in another template? Instead of re-creating the styles or macros in a different template, you can use the **Building Blocks Organizer** to copy these elements to a different template.

The Template Organizer

Word includes a template **Organizer** dialog box that you can use to copy styles and macros from one template to another. This capability comes in handy if you create a complex macro or custom style that you then want to use in other templates. If you want to make the style or macro available to any new document you create, add these elements to the Normal template. Word makes the settings in the Normal template available to new documents you create.

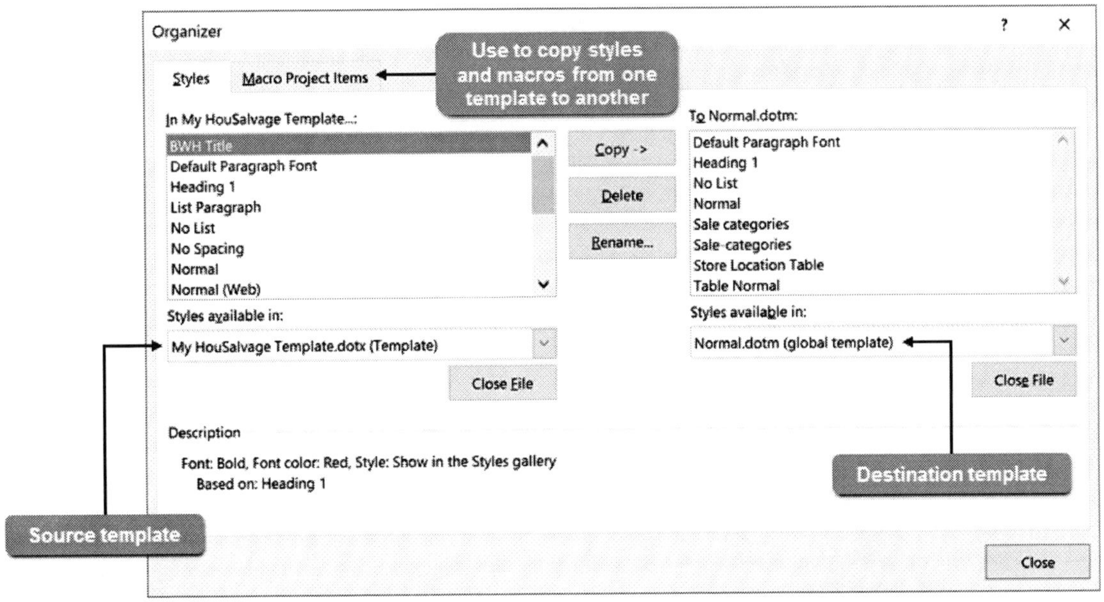

Figure 4-6: Use the Organizer dialog box to copy styles and macros from one template to another.

> **Note:** For more information, check out LearnTO **Share Templates with Other Users** from the **LearnTO** tile on your CHOICE Course screen.

> **Access the Checklist tile on your CHOICE Course screen for reference information and job aids on How to Manage Templates with the Template Organizer.**

ACTIVITY 4-4
Managing Templates with the Template Organizer

Before You Begin

You have created a custom template named My HouSalvage Template.dotx and stored it in the default Templates folder (**C:\Users**_username_**\Documents\Custom Office Templates**).

Scenario

You have created a custom template named My HouSalvage Template.dotx and stored it in the Custom Office Templates folder. You use the Building with Heart Title style and the Tagline style so frequently that you want to make these styles available in the Normal template. Adding these styles to the Normal template will enable you to use them in every new document you create.

---

1. Open the template you created named **My HouSalvage Template.dotx**.
   a) In Word, select **File→Open**.
   b) Select **Browse** and browse to the location **C:\Users**_username_**\Documents\Custom Office Templates**.
   c) Select **My HouSalvage Template.dotx** and then select **Open**. Word opens the template so that you can modify it.

2. Open the template **Organizer** dialog box.
   a) Select **File→Options** to open the **Word Options** dialog box.
   b) In the left pane, select the **Add-ins** category.
   c) From the **Manage** drop-down list, select **Templates**.

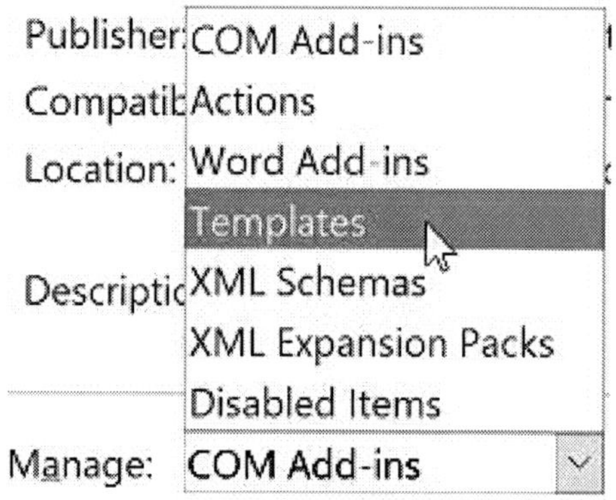

   d) Select **Go** to open the **Templates and Add-ins** dialog box.

---

e) In the lower-left corner of the **Templates and Add-ins** dialog box, select **Organizer** to open the **Organizer** dialog box.

The **Organizer** dialog box lists the styles in the My HouSalvage Template on the left side of the dialog box. On the right side of the dialog box, you see the styles in the Normal template.

3. Copy the **BWH Title** and **Tagline** styles to the Normal template.
   a) On the left side of the **Organizer** dialog box, select **BWH Title**.

   b) In the middle of the **Organizer** dialog box, select **Copy** to copy this style to the Normal template.

   c) Copy the **Tagline** style from My HouSalvage Template to the Normal template.
   d) Select **Close** to close the template **Organizer** dialog box.

4. Verify that the styles from My HouSalvage Template are now available in documents you create based on the Normal template.
   a) Close **My HouSalvage Template.dotx**.
   b) Select **File→New** and then select **Blank document** to create a new document based on the Normal template.
   c) On the **Home** tab, in the **Styles** group, select the Dialog Box Launcher to display the **Styles** pane.
   d) Verify that you see the **BWH Title** and the **Tagline** styles listed. These styles are available because you copied them from your document template to the Normal template.

5. Close Word.

Summary

In this lesson, you used templates to improve your efficiency and create consistently formatted documents. You used existing templates and modified a document, then saved it as a template. Using templates enables you to create consistently formatted documents with ease.

What types of documents in your organization lend themselves to creating templates?

Will you create templates from scratch, or will you base them on existing documents or templates? Why?

Note: Check your CHOICE Course screen for opportunities to interact with your classmates, peers, and the larger CHOICE online community about the topics covered in this course or other topics you are interested in. From the Course screen you can also access available resources for a more continuous learning experience.

5 Controlling the Flow of a Document

Lesson Time: 45 minutes

Lesson Objectives

In this lesson, you will control the flow of a document. You will:

- Manage the position of paragraphs on the page.

- Use section breaks to control the flow of a document.

- Insert columns in a document.

- Link text boxes.

Lesson Introduction

You have added and edited several elements in your documents. There are times when you need to control how text flows from one page to the next so that it makes the content easier to read. You might also want to have different sections of the document formatted in different ways.

TOPIC A

Control Paragraph Flow

Sometimes, you might find that the last word or line of a paragraph falls on the next page, separated from the rest of the paragraph. This can make it difficult for the reader to follow the content. If you have graphics in your document, they might push your text where you don't want it to be. In this topic, you will see how you can control the paragraph flow with paragraph options.

Paragraph Flow Options

In the **Paragraph** dialog box, on the **Line and Page Breaks** tab, you can configure options to control how paragraphs flow in your document.

Pagination Option	Description
Widow/Orphan control	Prevents single lines from being displayed at the top or bottom of a page. *Widows* are single lines at the top of a page separated from the rest of the paragraph of which they are a part. *Orphans* are single lines at the bottom of the page separated from the rest of the paragraph of which they are a part.
Keep with next	Keeps the selected paragraph on the same page as the next paragraph. A heading paragraph should appear on the same page as the first paragraph under that heading, so this would be a good use for this option.
Keep lines together	Keeps the selected lines from being split over a page break. An example of where you would likely use this option is when you are making a comparison between two items that are on separate lines.
Page break before	Places the selected paragraph at the top of the page. This is useful if you want a heading to be at the top of the page and not somewhere in the middle of the page.

 Access the Checklist tile on your CHOICE Course screen for reference information and job aids on **How to Control Paragraph Flow.**

ACTIVITY 5-1
Controlling Paragraph Flow

Data File

Desktop\Building with Heart\Controlling the Flow of a Document\Preparation for new store openings.docx

Scenario

As the office manager for the HouSalvage main office, you have been working hard to prepare for the two new store openings. You put together a list of the things that need to be done in preparation for the grand openings. As the document stands right now, some of the paragraphs break across pages and a graphic is separated from the text that refers to it. You would like to make sure the content for each item in the list stays together on the same page.

---

1. Open the **Preparation for new store openings.docx** document and save it with a new name.
   a) From the **Desktop\Building with Heart\Controlling the Flow of a Document** folder, open the **Preparation for new store openings.docx** file.
   b) Save the file as *My preparation for new store openings.docx*

2. Configure paragraph flow options to keep the list item with the graphic on the same page.
   a) Scroll down so that you can see the bottom of page 1 and the top of page 2. Notice that the text that refers to the image of the Frequent Buyer Card is at the bottom of page 1 and the image of the card is on page 2.
   b) Select the text beginning with **5. Create customer loyalty program** down through the graphic.
   c) On the **Home** tab, in the **Paragraph** group, select the **Paragraph** Dialog Box Launcher.
   d) In the **Paragraph** dialog box, select the **Line and Page Breaks** tab.
   e) In the **Pagination** section, check **Keep with next**.
   f) Select **OK**.
   g) Verify that Word moved a portion of the first paragraph for item 5, the following paragraph, and the graphic to the same page now.

   opening packet includes an application for our Frequent Buyer Program if they are not already a member.

   This is an example of the Frequent Buyer Program card:

3. Configure paragraph flow so that the checklist appears on a separate page.

a) Scroll down to the checklist near the end of the document.
b) Position the insertion point in the word "Checklist."
c) Open the **Paragraph** dialog box.
d) On the **Line and Page Breaks** tab, in the **Pagination** section, select the **Page break before** check box.
e) Select **OK**.
f) Verify that the checklist is now on a separate page from the rest of the list items.
g) Save your changes and then close the file.

TOPIC B

Insert Section Breaks

You have seen how to control the flow of paragraph text in a document. You might need to control how larger sections of a document flow. You can accomplish this by breaking the document into sections, which you will do in this topic.

You might need different page layouts for different parts of a document. For example, you might need different margin widths or page orientations. Inserting section breaks enables you to have multiple layouts within a single document.

Sections and Section Breaks

A *section break* divides a document into sections where a different page layout can be configured for each section of the document. Without section breaks, the same page layout configuration is applied to the whole document. The page layout includes headers, footers, page numbering, page orientation, and margins. If you want section breaks, you must insert them manually.

Section Titles

Using titles for sections helps make the document more easily navigable for those individuals using adaptive technologies such as screen readers. When the screen reader encounters titles and headings, it makes it easier for the reader to navigate to the correct section so that the document can be read in the correct order.

Types of Section Breaks

There are four types of section breaks you can insert in a Word document.

Figure 5-1: There are four types of section breaks.

The following table describes each type of section break.

Section Break Type	Description
Next Page	A new section is created that starts on the next page. With this type of section break, you can apply different page numbers, headers, footers, page orientation, paper size, and vertical alignment to the sections in the document.
Continuous	The new section starts on the same page where you insert the section break. However, if the sections before and after the section break are configured for different page sizes or page orientation, the new section will begin on a new page. With this type of section break, you can apply different column formatting or margins on the same page. If the section above the section break contains multiple columns, the columns are balanced above the section break and then the new section begins.
Even Page	The new section starts on the next even-numbered page. If the section break is inserted on an even-numbered page, a blank page is inserted for the odd-numbered page so that the new section will begin on an even-numbered page.

Section Break Type	Description
Odd Page	The new section starts on the next odd-numbered page. If the section break is inserted on an odd-numbered page, a blank page is inserted for the even-numbered page so that the new section will begin on an odd-numbered page. **Odd Page** section breaks are often used for documents containing chapters so that the chapter begins on the right-hand side of a book that is bound in the center.

When to Use Section Breaks

What if you're creating a document and you want to use Roman numerals for the first several pages and then switch to traditional page numbering? Or what if your document contains a table that is too wide for printing with portrait orientation? As mentioned, you can configure different page layouts as well as headers and footers for each section in your document. You create a section in a document by inserting a section break. The default behavior in Word is to use the same page layout, page orientation, and headers and footers as the previous section. You can configure a new page layout and page orientation in a new section.

To use a different header and/or footer than the previous section, you need to unlink the header or footer from the previous section and create new headers and/or footers for the new section. By default, headers and footers are linked to the previous section so the headers and footers carry over into the new section.

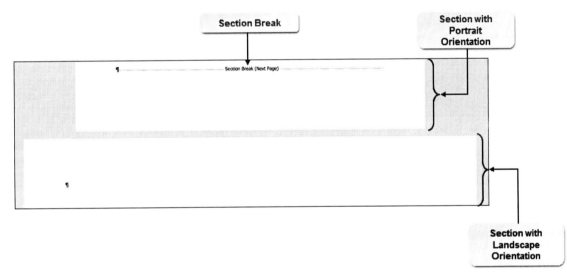

Figure 5-2: Use a section break to create a section in your document with landscape page orientation.

	Access the Checklist tile on your CHOICE Course screen for reference information and job aids on **How to Insert Section Breaks**.

ACTIVITY 5-2
Inserting Section Breaks

Data File

Desktop\Building with Heart\Controlling the Flow of a Document\HouSalvage Newsletter.docx

Scenario

You have gathered the items for the newsletter and need to format it. The content is currently just in blocks of text. You would like the newsletter title to fit on one line. You would like headers and footers on all pages except the first page.

---

1. Open the **HouSalvage Newsletter.docx** document and save it with a new name.

   a) From the **Desktop\Building with Heart\Controlling the Flow of a Document** folder, open the **HouSalvage Newsletter.docx** document.

   b) Save the file as *My HouSalvage Newsletter.docx*

2. Observe the format of the first page of the newsletter. The content below the heading "HouSalvage Recycling Centers Open New Store" is contained in two columns; the rest of the content on page one is in a single column that is the width of the page.

3. Observe what happens if you delete a section break.

   a) If paragraph marks and other formatting symbols are not visible in the document, on the **Home** tab, in the **Paragraph** group, select **Show/Hide ¶**.

   b) Observe the section break to the right of the heading "HouSalvage Recycling Centers Open New Store." This section break makes it possible for the document to have two columns below this heading.

HouSalvage·Recycling·Centers·Open·New·Store¶ ····Section Break (Continuous)····

Your·favorite·store·is·opening·a·new·location·in·
South·Greene!·You,·our·loyal·customers,·have·

provided·incentives·to·get·those·properties·back·
in·use·and·we·loved·both·the·locations·and·the·

   c) Observe the section break at the end of the second column. Word displays this section break simply as a dotted line.

South·Greene·this·month.·Next·month,·another·
new·store·opens·in·Riverside.·¶

We·are·taking·over·two·of·the·manufacturing·
sites·that·closed·several·years·ago.·The·city·

manufacturing·sites·to·retail·space,·but·it·was·
worth·the·effort.·We're·sure·you·will·agree·when·
you·see·the·spacious·new·stores!·

d) Delete the first section break (the one that displays "Section Break (Continuous)"). Observe the results.

OCTOBER·5,·2015¶
VOLUME·1,·ISSUE·1

ʺHouSalvage·Recycling·
Centers·Open·New·Store¶
Your·favorite·store·is·opening·a·new·location·in·
South·Greene!·You,·our·loyal·customers,·have·

We·are·taking·over·two·of·the·manufacturing·
sites·that·closed·several·years·ago.·The·city·
provided·incentives·to·get·those·properties·back·
in·use·and·we·loved·both·the·locations·and·the·
buildings.·They·are·big·enough·to·allow·us·to·
expand·our·merchandise·offerings·and·they·are·
located·in·the·fast·growing·Greene·suburbs·¶

Word applies the two-column format to all the content that precedes the section break at the end of the "HouSalvage Recycling Centers Open New Store" section.

e) Press **Ctrl+Z** to undo the deletion of the first section break.

4. Create narrower margins for the heading of the newsletter so that "HouSalvage Recycling Centers" and the tagline fit to the right of the Building with Heart logo.

   a) Position the cursor at the end of the "Volume 1, Issue 1" line.

   b) On the **Layout** tab, in the **Page Setup** group, select **Breaks**.

   c) Select **Continuous**. This creates a section break after the "Volume 1, Issue 1" line so that you can change the margins of the header without affecting the rest of the document.

   d) With the cursor after "Issue 1" and above the section break, on the **Layout** tab, in the **Page Setup** group, select **Margins**.

   e) Select **Narrow**.

   f) Verify that the heading now fits on a single line and that the rest of the document still has the original margin width.

¶
·HouSalvage·Recycling·Centers¶
Your·source·for·recycled·construction·materials·since·1995¶

SEPTEMBER·8,·2015¶
VOLUME·1,·ISSUE·1

·····································Section Break (Continuous)·····································

5. Create custom margins for the "About Building with Heart" portion of the document to make room for the text box at the bottom of page 4.

   a) Scroll to page 4. Position the cursor at the beginning of the line "About Building with Heart."

   b) On the **Layout** tab, in the **Page Setup** group, select **Breaks**.

   c) Select **Next Page**.

   d) With the cursor after the new section break, on the **Layout** tab, in the **Page Setup** group, select **Margins**.

   e) Select **Custom Margins**.

f) In the **Page Setup** dialog box, on the **Margins** tab, change the **Right** margin to **2.25"**.

Page Setup   ?   ✕

Margins	Paper	Layout

Margins

<u>T</u>op:	1"		<u>B</u>ottom:	1"
<u>L</u>eft:	1"		<u>R</u>ight:	2.25"
<u>G</u>utter:	0"		G<u>u</u>tter position:	Left

g) Select **OK**.

h) If necessary, reposition the pull quote text box to fit on the right side of the "About Building with Heart" portion of the document.

i) Position the cursor at the beginning of the line "Employee of the Month."

j) Insert a **Continuous** section break.

k) Set the margins to **Normal**.

6. Add headers and footers to all sections except those on the first page.

a) Scroll to page 2.

b) Double-click the top margin of the second page to open the header area.

c) On the **Header & Footer Tools Design** tab, in the **Navigation** group, deselect **Link to Previous** to turn off header linking.

d) Type *HouSalvage Recycling Centers News* and then press **Tab** twice.

e) On the **Insert** tab, in the **Text** group, select **Date & Time**.

f) Select the third date type and then select **OK**.

g) On the **Header & Footer Tools Design** tab, in the **Navigation** group, select **Go to Footer** to display the footer area on page 2.

h) On the **Header & Footer Tools Design** tab, in the **Navigation** group, deselect **Link to Previous** to turn off footer linking.

i) On the **Insert** tab, in the **Header & Footer group**, select **Page Number**.

j) Point to the **Bottom of Page** gallery and then in the gallery, select **Brackets 2**.

k) Scroll through the document to verify that the first page has no header or footer and that there are headers and footers on the rest of the pages.

l) Save the file.

TOPIC C

Insert Columns

You have added section breaks to a document to allow different margin widths on different parts of a document. Column breaks are another type of break. They allow the text to flow in multiple columns on a page. This is the type of break you will insert in this topic.

Using columns in documents such as newsletters allows readers to more easily read the content. Columns break the content into chunks that the eye can easily digest without excessive lateral movement, so the readers don't lose their place.

Text Columns

Columns are a page layout feature that enables you to place multiple columns of text on the page. When one column is filled, the text automatically flows to the next column. If the last column on the page is filled, the text automatically flows to the next page in the first column. Paragraph flow settings work the same way across column breaks as they do across page breaks. You can insert a column break to force the text to the next column. The entire document can be formatted as columns, or you can create columns in a section of the document.

You can place content other than just text in columns. You can add images, tables, and bulleted and numbered lists.

■ **Pet·Department·in·New·Stores¶**----------------Section Break (Continuous)----------------

With·the·additional·space· available·in·the·new·stores·in· South·Greene·and·Riverside,· we·will·be·adding·a·pet· department.·We·will·have· pet·supplies,·pet·food,·and· on·the·weekends,·the·local· animal·shelters·will·be· bringing·in·pets·available·for· adoption.·HouSalvage·has· always·supported·the·local· animal·shelters.·¶

----------Column Break----------

Well·behaved·dogs·and· other·animals·on·leads·are· always·welcome·in·any·of· our·stores.·If·your·dog·needs· training,·our·new·pet· department·has·a·separate· room·where·our·new·trainers· will·offer·classes·to·help·your· dog·learn·good·manners.·· Dogs·will·learn·the·basic· obedience·commands·like· sit,·stay,·come,·down;·they· will·also·learn·useful· commands·such·as·leave·it,· drop·it,·back,·and·wait.¶

Column Break

If·there·is·enough·interest,· we·will·also·be·adding·agility· classes·soon.·If·your·dog· loves·to·run·and·jump,·this·is· a·fun·sport·for·you·and·your· dog·to·get·exercise·and·form· a·special·bond.¶

Our·trainers·are·certified· through·either·the· Certification·Council·for· Professional·Dog·Trainers· (CCPDT)·or·the·Association·of· Pet·Dog·Trainers·(APDT).· They·trained·both·Bob·and· Emily,·and·look·how·well· behaved·they·both·are!¶

■ **Contest¶**

Help·us·name·Bob·and·Emily's·puppies·when·they·arrive.·In·addition·to·naming·the·puppies,·other·prizes· will·be·awarded·for·silliest·names,·most·unusual·names,·and·more!·¶

Figure 5–3: Columns with column breaks in a section of a document.

Text Column Options

The **Columns** gallery contains predefined column settings. You can select one, two, or three evenly spaced, same-width columns. The gallery also has settings for a wide left and narrow right column, and vice versa. If you want more columns, to change the width or spacing, or to add a line between columns, from the **Columns** menu, select **More Columns**. Word displays the **Columns** dialog box.

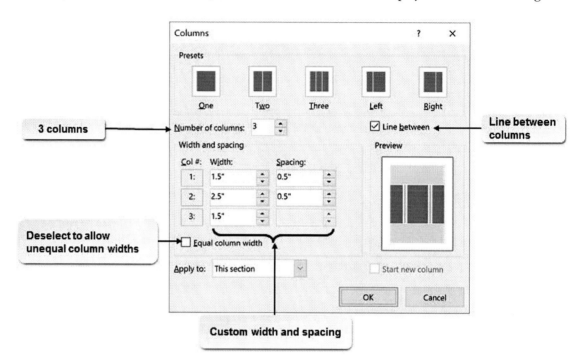

Figure 5-4: The Columns dialog box with custom options set.

In the **Columns** dialog box, the maximum **Number of columns** setting you can configure is nine. The **Apply to** option allows you to specify whether columns are applied to the **Selected text**, **Selected sections**, or the **Whole document**.

> Access the Checklist tile on your CHOICE Course screen for reference information and job aids on How to Insert Columns.

ACTIVITY 5-3
Inserting Columns

Before You Begin
The My HouSalvage Newsletter.docx document is open.

Scenario
Because this is a newsletter, you want to use columns to make it look more traditional. There is some information that you want to stay at full width, some that you think would work well in three columns, and some that you think would work better with a wide column next to a narrow column. You are aware that you might need to add column breaks or move text to make it more readable.

1. Format the first story in the newsletter as three columns.
   a) On the first page, select the four paragraphs of text under the heading "HouSalvage Recycling Centers Open New Store."
   b) On the **Layout** tab, in the **Page Setup** group, select **Columns**.
   c) Select **Three** to convert the text to three columns.
   d) Observe that Word formatted only the text you selected into columns.

2. Format the "DIY Seminars" section with custom column widths, with the list of seminars in the right column.
   a) Scroll down to page 2 and select the text under the "DIY Seminars" heading. This includes three paragraphs of text and a bulleted list.
   b) On the **Layout** tab, in the **Page Setup** group, select **Columns**.
   c) Select **More Columns**.
   d) In the **Columns** dialog box, configure your columns as shown:

   e) Verify that **Apply to** is set to **Selected text**.
   f) Select **OK**.
   g) Notice that the right column has more content than the left column. You can adjust this by inserting a column break. Position the cursor just before "Some of the seminars."

> **Note:** Alternatively, you can press **Ctrl+Shift+Enter** to insert a column break.

h) On the **Layout** tab, in the **Page Setup** group, select **Breaks→Column**.

• **DIY·Seminars**————————————————Section Break (Continuous)————————————————

Do·you·want·to·save·money·by·doing·home·repairs·and·fix·ups·yourself?·Our·Do·It·Yourself·(DIY)·seminars·are·the·first·step·to·getting·there.·Most·seminars·are·free,·but·for·some·there·is·a·small·cost·to·cover·materials.·No·more·cramped·quarters·in·a·corner·of·the·store·for·these·training·sessions.·Our·new·stores·have·fully·equipped·training·rooms·with·tools,·workbenches,·and·high-back·stools·for·your·comfort·at·your·spacious·workstation.·¶

Register·today·as·seating·is·limited.·Most·seminars·are·1·hour·long,·but·some·are·longer.·Check·the·in-store·schedule·for·times·and·dates.¶

Some·of·the·seminars·we·have·planned·are:¶

- • Changing·the·faucet·on·your·sink¶
- • Clearing·drain·lines¶
- • Building·a·bird·house¶
- • Hanging·wallpaper¶
- • Painting·inside·and·out¶
- • Lawn·care·101¶
- • Decorating·for·the·holidays¶
  - ○ Varies·by·the·next·holiday·on·the·calendar¶
- • Picking·gifts·for·your·special·handyman·or·handywoman¶
- • Ladder·safety¶————Section Break (Continuous)————

i) Save the file.

TOPIC D

Link Text Boxes to Control Text Flow

So far, you have controlled text flow using section breaks, columns, and column breaks. Another way you can control text flow is to link text boxes together, which is what you will do in this topic.

If you think of newsletters, they usually have several lead stories on the first page; the rest of the content for the article is located elsewhere in the newsletter. Linked text boxes allow you to do this in Word.

Linked Text Boxes

You can link two or more *text boxes* so that Word automatically displays the text that overflows the first text box in any linked text boxes. This is useful if you want text to appear on one page of a document, such as the first page of a newsletter, and the rest of the story to appear on a later page. When you select the box to link from and select the option to create the link, the cursor changes to an upright container. When you select the box to which you want to link the text, the cursor changes to a container with letters flowing out of it.

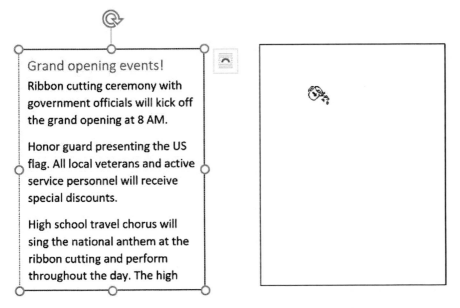

Figure 5-5: Linked text boxes allow text to begin in a text box on one page and continue in a text box on another page.

Insert Text from a File

You can insert the text from one file into another file. Select **Insert→Text→Object→Text from File**. You can insert the text into the document or into a text box in the document.

> Access the Checklist tile on your CHOICE Course screen for reference information and job aids on **How to Link Text Boxes to Control Text Flow**.

ACTIVITY 5-4
Linking Text Boxes to Control Text Flow

Data File

Desktop\Building with Heart\Controlling the Flow of a Document\Grand opening events.docx

Before You Begin

My HouSalvage Newsletter.docx is open.

Scenario

The store manager for the new South Greene store just sent you a list of events that will take place during the grand opening of her store. You think it would make a great first-page story in the HouSalvage Newsletter, but you already have the text that fills most of the page. You think it would work well to start the story about the grand opening events on the first page and finish it on the last page, which still has lots of open space.

1. In the newsletter, create a text box at the bottom of page 1 and insert the text from the **Grand opening events.docx** file in the text box.

   a) Scroll to the bottom of the first page of **My HouSalvage Newsletter.docx**.

   b) On the **Insert** tab, in the **Text** group, select **Text Box**.

   c) Select **Draw Text Box**.

   d) To the right of the "We are hiring" list, drag to create a text box large enough to hold some text. This is where you will insert the first part of the story.

   e) On the **Insert** tab, in the **Text** group, from the **Object** drop-down list, select **Text from File**.

   f) In the **Insert File** dialog box, navigate to the **Desktop\Building with Heart\Controlling the Flow of a Document** folder and select **Grand opening events.docx**.

   g) Select **Insert**. The text is too long to fit in the text box.

2. Create a text box on page 5 of the newsletter and link it to the text box on page 1.

   a) Scroll to the end of the document.

   b) Draw a text box across the width of the page and approximately two inches high.

   c) Scroll up to page 1 and click in the text box.

   d) On the **Drawing Tools Format** tab, in the **Text** group, select **Create Link**. Notice that the cursor changes to a full container.

   e) Jump to page 5 again and move your cursor over the text box you inserted at the bottom of the page. Notice that the cursor changes to a container spilling letters.

   f) Click the text box to create the link. Word "pours" the rest of the content into the second text box.

   g) Adjust the sizes of the two text boxes to see how Word moves the text between them.

   h) Adjust the Word zoom level so that you can see all five pages simultaneously. Notice that the content now fills both text boxes.

   i) Return the Word zoom level to **100%**.

   j) Add a text box below the first text box and enter the text *Continued on Page 5*

   k) Add a text box above the second text box at the end of the document and enter the text *Continued from Page 1*

   l) Save and close the file and close Word.

Summary

In this lesson, you controlled the flow of a document in various ways. You controlled how text flows between paragraphs. You inserted section breaks to enable different page layouts for various parts of the document. You inserted columns in your document and inserted column breaks to control the flow of text between columns. You also linked two text boxes together so that text overflowed from the first text box into the second text box. Now that you can control the flow of text throughout your document, you will simplify and manage long documents.

In what ways will you use paragraph and page text flow control features in your documents?

What text flow features might you use when creating a newsletter?

 Note: Check your CHOICE Course screen for opportunities to interact with your classmates, peers, and the larger CHOICE online community about the topics covered in this course or other topics you are interested in. From the Course screen you can also access available resources for a more continuous learning experience.

6 Simplifying and Managing Long Documents

Lesson Time: 1 hour

Lesson Objectives

In this lesson, you will simplify and manage long documents. You will:

- Insert blank and cover pages.

- Create an index.

- Create a table of contents.

- Create an ancillary table.

- Manage the outlines of complex documents.

- Create and manage a master document.

Lesson Introduction

When you work with a document in Microsoft® Word, you can use features such as the **Navigation** pane to simplify navigating through a document. Locating information in a lengthy printed document is more difficult. To help the reader of a print copy of a document, you can create a list of relevant items or key words. In this lesson, you will generate and insert reference lists in a document.

TOPIC A

Insert Blank and Cover Pages

You manipulated the flow of content in a document by using section breaks, page breaks, columns, and column breaks. A cover page and carefully placed blank pages provide the reader with a professional-looking document as well as a visual pause between reading sections.

The packaging of an item on a store shelf is not just a container; it also helps to sell the product. In the same fashion, a well-designed cover page gives your document a professional look and makes it more appealing. Word offers a range of built-in choices to help you create and format your cover pages. Inserting blank pages at strategic locations helps to break up large blocks of text and visually separate major sections.

Cover and Blank Pages

A *cover page* is an attractive first page containing information such as the title, author's name, and date. The **Cover Page** gallery provides a diverse selection of built-in cover pages. Each cover page style includes standard fields for customizing text. You insert the cover page at the beginning of a document before the first page. You can also insert blank pages quickly to break up the monotony of lengthy text or to differentiate major sections of a document.

 Access the Checklist tile on your CHOICE Course screen for reference information and job aids on How to Insert Cover and Blank Pages.

ACTIVITY 6-1
Inserting Cover and Blank Pages

Data File

Desktop\Building with Heart\Simplifying and Managing Long Documents\Building with Heart Proposal.docx

Scenario

Greene City has sent out a request for proposals (RFP) for construction companies to bid on creating a new neighborhood for low- and very low-income residents. A coworker has started Building with Heart's proposal for this project. You have been asked to make the proposal look more professional. First, you want to add and modify a cover page so that the document meets the city's requirements. Then, you will add a blank page after the cover page.

1. Open the **Desktop\Building with Heart\Simplifying and Managing Long Documents\Building with Heart Proposal.docx** document and save it with a new name.
    a) In the **Desktop\Building with Heart\Simplifying and Managing Long Documents** folder, open the **Building with Heart Proposal** document.
    b) Save the document as *My Building with Heart Proposal*

2. Insert a cover page.
    a) Position the insertion point at the beginning of the "EXECUTIVE SUMMARY" section.
    b) On the **Insert** tab, in the **Pages** group, select **Cover Page**.
    c) From the **Built-in** gallery, select **Filigree**.

     Note: By default, the Filigree cover page converts what you type to uppercase letters.

    d) Click in the field **[Document title]** and type *Response to RFP # 2016901*
    e) Click in the **[Document subtitle]** field, and type *Greene City River Subdivision*
    f) Select the **Date** field, and then select the drop-down arrow next to it and select a date from the displayed calendar.
    g) In the **Company Name** field, type *Building with Heart*
    h) Right-click the **Company address** field and select **Remove Content Control**.
    i) Change the cover page to a different cover page in the **Cover Page** gallery.
       Notice that the fields that are common to both cover pages are already filled in.
    j) Change the cover page back to **Filigree**. Remove the **Company address** field.

3. Insert a blank page after the cover page.
    a) Click in the cover page away from any of the fields.
    b) On the **Insert** tab, in the **Pages** group, select **Blank Page**. Word inserts a blank page after the cover page.

     Note: Note that when the cursor is in any of the fields on the cover page, in the **Pages** group, the **Blank Page** button is not available.

    c) Save your changes.

TOPIC B

Insert an Index

A cover page and well-placed blank pages add a professional touch. Providing a detailed listing of the important terms and concepts in the document along with their page numbers will help the reader locate information. In this topic, you will insert an index.

An index enables the reader to locate entries you have marked in a document. Instead of the reader paging through the document looking for specific material, the index provides a quick way to find the information. When you use Word to create the index, the index automatically updates whenever the document text or pagination changes.

The Index Dialog Box

The **Index** dialog box enables you to insert, format, and modify the index in a document.

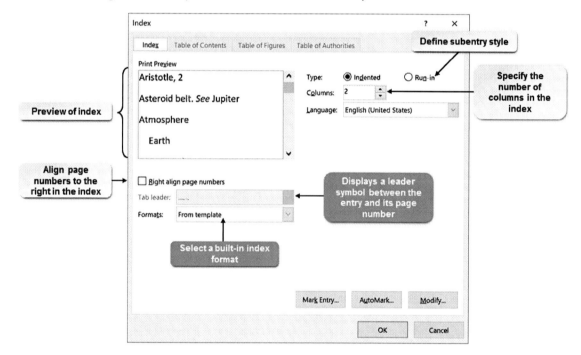

Figure 6–1: The Index dialog box.

The following table describes the options available in the **Index** dialog box.

Option	Enables You To
Print Preview	Preview the index as it would appear in the printed document.
Type	Choose whether the index subentry text is indented below the main entry or run in as continuous entries.
Columns	Select the number of columns the index will contain.
Language	Set the desired language for the index entry.
Right align page numbers	Align the index page numbers along the right margin of the page.

Option	Enables You To
Tab leader	Set a tab leader or change the type of leader symbol. This option is available when the **Right align page numbers** check box is checked.
Formats	Select a built-in index format.
Mark Entry	Access the **Mark Index Entry** dialog box, which you can use to find and mark text as index entries.
AutoMark	Mark new entries automatically using a concordance file.
Modify	Access the **Style** dialog box to format the text entries in the index.

> **Note:** The **Indented** option is the default and lists the marked content based on a hierarchy. If you select **Run-in**, Word displays the content as continuous text with one entry following another on the same line.

Index Entry Field Codes

When you mark an index entry, Word represents the entry by a field code. You can display the field code by enabling the **Show All Formatting Marks** option in the **Word Options** dialog box or by selecting the **Show/Hide ¶** button in the **Paragraph** group on the **Home** tab. The field code displays the index entry within quotes, and the term "XE" precedes the index entry. To edit the index entry without making changes to the field code, you need to change only the text within the quotes in the field code.

Subentries

An index often contains a main entry and one or more subentries. The main entries could be the headings in a document, while the subentries point to other related information that the reader may want to investigate.

The Mark Index Entry Dialog Box

In the **Index** dialog box, selecting **Mark Entry** opens the **Mark Index Entry** dialog box, which contains options used to create and mark text as index entries. You can mark one instance of an entry or have Word mark all instances of that entry. After you mark an entry, the dialog box remains open so you can easily mark another entry.

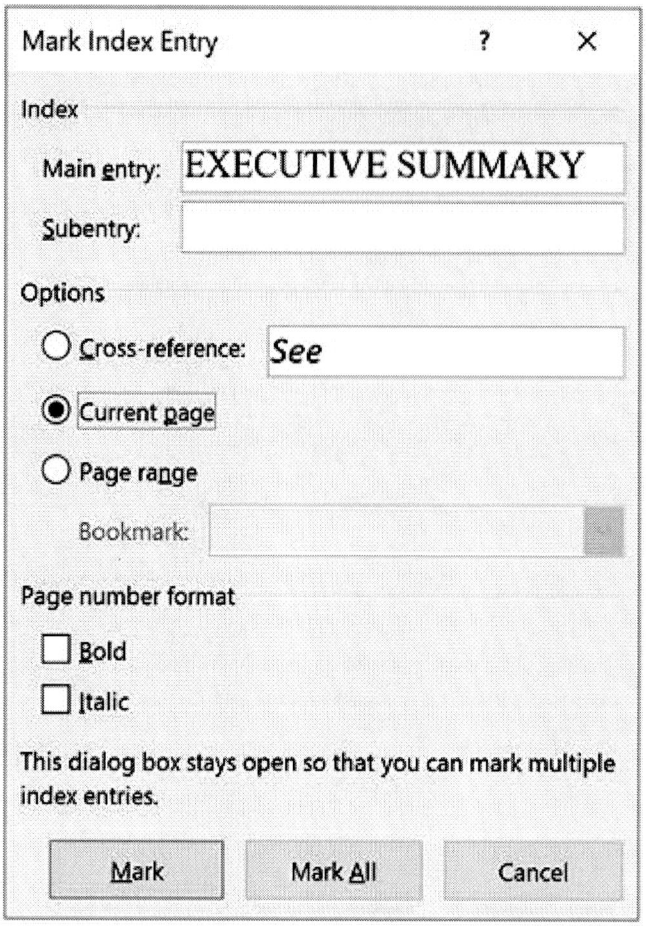

Figure 6–2: Use the Mark Index Entry dialog box to add terms to the index.

The following table describes the sections of the **Mark Index Entry** dialog box.

Panel	Enables You To
Index	Specify the main index entry text and subentries.
Options	Specify the type of index entry.
Page number format	Select a format for the page numbers in the index.

Mark Index Entries Options

By default, index entries use the **Current page** option to identify the marked term or phrase on a particular page. The **Cross-reference** option allows you to redirect the reader to another term in the index. The **Page range** options allow you to type or select a bookmark from the **Bookmark** drop-down list. For example, if a reader looks up the word "desk" in an index, you might use the **Cross-reference** option to insert "See Furniture" to redirect the reader to the "Furniture" index entry.

The Open Index AutoMark File Dialog Box

In the **Index** dialog box, selecting **AutoMark** displays the **Open Index AutoMark File** dialog box. This dialog box enables you to navigate to a concordance file. Opening the concordance file through this dialog box automatically marks the text in the concordance file as index entries in the current document and closes the dialog box. Only the first occurrence of each entry in a paragraph is marked.

The Concordance File

A *concordance file* is a document containing a two-column table Word uses to automatically mark index entries in another document. You can use a concordance file with many similar documents to quickly index the bulk of the text. You can then manually mark any index entries for text that is not included in the concordance file.

The first column of the concordance table lists the terms and phrases in the document you want to mark as index entries. The text in the first column must match exactly how the text appears in the document you want to index. The second column contains the actual index entries for the text in the first column. Each table cell must contain only one entry.

Greene City River	Greene City River
efficiencies	efficiency
Patio homes	efficiency: patio homes
patio homes	efficiency: patio homes
low income	income requirement
Low-Income	income requirement
very low-income	income requirement
Very Low-Income	income requirement
workshops	services
countertop	home customizations: countertop
cabinets	home customizations: cabinets
flooring	home customizations: flooring
paint	home customizations: paint
financial stability	financial information
expenses	financial information: expenses
Mission Statement	mission statement
Key Personnel	key personnel

Left column contains text as it appears in the document

Right column contains entries and subentries as they will appear in the index

Figure 6–3: A concordance table.

The Style Dialog Box

In the **Index** dialog box, selecting **Modify** opens the **Style** dialog box, which contains various options you can use to format the index style.

Option	Description
Styles	Displays a list of built-in index styles available in the document.
Preview	Displays a preview of the selected style.
Modify	Displays the **Modify Style** dialog box, which you use to adjust the selected index style.

The Modify Style Dialog Box

In the **Style** dialog box, selecting **Modify** displays the **Modify Style** dialog box, with additional options you can use to format an index.

Option	Enables You To
Properties	View the name of the selected index style, type of style, origin format, and the style for the paragraph following an index entry.
Formatting	Format an index entry by specifying the font, font size, font styles, and font color.
Alignment	Format the text alignment, spacing, and indentation of an index entry.
Preview	Preview the formatting choices for an index entry.
Add to Quick Style list	Add the current formatting as a style in the **Quick Style** list.
Automatically update	Automatically update the formatting style of the entries in other indices.
Only in this document	Specify the formatting options for the current document only.
New documents based on this template	Set the current index entries format as a template for use in other documents.

The Navigation Pane

The **Navigation** pane appears to the left of the document and enables users to quickly navigate to a desired location. By default, the pane displays any headings and subheadings in the document to which you have applied a Heading style. You can also use the **Navigation** pane to browse by pages, or use the pane to search for text in the document. To display the **Navigation** pane, on the **View** tab, in the **Show** group, check the **Navigation Pane** check box.

 Access the Checklist tile on your CHOICE Course screen for reference information and job aids on How to Mark Index Entries.

 Access the Checklist tile on your CHOICE Course screen for reference information and job aids on How to Index a Document.

ACTIVITY 6-2
Indexing a Document

Data File

Desktop\Building with Heart\Simplifying and Managing Long Documents\Proposal Concordance.docx

Before You Begin

My Building with Heart Proposal.docx is open.

Scenario

One of the requirements in the Greene City Council's RFP is that proposals must include an index. Also, you know that adding an index will help the reader to quickly find information in the proposal. You will manually mark a few words and generate the index. Then you will use an existing concordance file to add more entries to the index. To navigate through the document, you display the **Navigation** pane.

---

1. Display the **Mark Index Entry** dialog box.
   a) On the **View** tab, in the **Show** group, check the **Navigation Pane** check box.
   b) In the **Navigation** pane, select the heading **EXECUTIVE SUMMARY** to navigate to the page.
   c) Select the heading **EXECUTIVE SUMMARY**.
   d) On the **References** tab, in the **Index** group, select **Mark Entry**.
   e) In the **Mark Index Entry** dialog box, select **Mark**. Notice that Word automatically enables the display of format marks. The **Mark Index Entry** dialog box remains open.

2. Add a second index entry.
   a) In the second paragraph on the same page, select the words **Request for Proposals (RFP)**.
   b) In the **Mark Index Entry** dialog box, click in the **Main entry** text box. Word inserts the selected text into the text box.
   c) Select **Mark**.

3. Mark all instances of a word.
   a) In the last sentence on page 3, select the lowercase words **low-income**.
   b) In the **Mark Index Entry** dialog box, click in the **Main entry** text box.
   c) Select **Mark All**, and then select **Close**.

4. Examine a concordance file.
   a) In the **Desktop\Building with Heart\Simplifying and Managing Long Documents** folder, open the file **Proposal Concordance.docx**.
   b) Examine the table entries. The left column contains text as it appears in the document. The right column contains entries and subentries as they will appear in the index.
   c) Close the document.

5. Automatically mark entries using a concordance file.
   a) On the **References** tab, in the **Index** group, select **Insert Index**.
   b) In the **Index** dialog box, select **AutoMark**.
   c) Locate and select the file **Proposal Concordance.docx** and select **Open**. The **Open Index AutoMark File** dialog box closes.

6. Insert and format the index.

   a) Using the **Navigation** pane, select the document heading **INDEX**.

   b) Place the insertion point in the line below this heading.

   c) On the **References** tab, in the **Index** group, select **Insert Index**.

   d) In the **Index** dialog box, from the **Formats** drop-down list, select **Modern**.

   e) Select **OK**. The entries you marked along with the entries from the concordance file are listed in the index.

   f) Save the document.

Note: On the **Home** tab, in the **Paragraph** group, select **Show/Hide ¶** to turn off the display of formatting marks so that you can get a better sense of how the document looks.

TOPIC C

Insert a Table of Contents

Inserting an index enables the reader to find specific terms or subjects in a long document. Another helpful reference table you commonly see in documents is a table of contents. The table of contents is a comprehensive list of topics in the document. In this topic, you will insert a table of contents in the document.

Most readers don't have time to read every book or report cover to cover. The table of contents helps the reader quickly find the topics they want without leafing through the whole document. It can also give the reader an idea of what major topics are covered in the text. Like other reference tables in Word, the table of contents remains up-to-date whenever the document's text or pagination changes.

Table of Contents

A table of contents (TOC) is a list of headings with corresponding page numbers. When the table of contents is generated, any text formatted using the built-in Heading styles is automatically included in the listing. Word indents the headings based on the Heading style of the text.

The Table of Contents Dialog Box

The **Table of Contents** dialog box contains options to insert, format, and modify a table of contents.

Option	Enables You To
Print Preview	Preview how the table of contents appears in the printed document.
Web Preview	Preview how the table of contents appears on a web page.
Show page numbers	Display or suppress the page numbers in the table of contents.
Right align page numbers	Align the page numbers along the right margin of the page.
Tab leader	Set the tab leader format for the page numbers.
Use hyperlinks instead of page numbers	Preview the listed page references in the table of contents as hyperlinks. The user can select the desired link to navigate to a specific page.
Formats	Format the table of contents using preset formats.
Show levels	Determine the number of levels listed in the table of contents.
Options	Display the **Table of Contents Options** dialog box, in which you can modify the styles included in the table of contents.
Modify	Display the **Style** dialog box, in which you can modify the style of the table of contents.

The Add Text Option

On the **References** tab, in the **Table of Contents** group, you can use the **Add Text** drop-down list to add an entry to the table of contents by selecting the text in the document and then choosing its hierarchy level.

Option	Description
Do Not Show in Table of Contents	Does not display the selected text in the table of contents. This applies the Normal style to the selected text.
Level 1	Displays the selected text at the first level of the hierarchy. This applies the Heading 1 style to the selected text.
Level 2	Displays the selected text at the second level of the hierarchy. This applies the Heading 2 style to the selected text.
Level 3	Displays the selected text at the third level of the hierarchy. This applies the Heading 3 style to the selected text.

The Mark Table of Contents Entry Dialog Box

If you need to insert text or a heading in a table of contents and do not want to reformat the text with standard Heading styles, you can manually mark the headings you want to include.

The **Mark Table of Contents Entry** dialog box contains options to manually mark text as an entry for the table of contents.

Option	Description
Entry	Displays the text to be marked as an entry for the table of contents.
Table identifier	Enables Word to identify the table of contents based on hierarchy. This is set to **C** if there is no other reference table in the document.
Level	Enables you to select a level for this table of contents entry.
Mark	Marks the text with the specified settings as a table of contents entry.

Access the Checklist tile on your CHOICE Course screen for reference information and job aids on How to Insert a Table of Contents.

ACTIVITY 6–3
Inserting a Table of Contents

Before You Begin
My Building with Heart Proposal.docx is open.

Scenario
Another Greene City Council requirement is that you must include a table of contents in your proposal. Because the document headings have Heading styles applied, it should be easy to generate the table of contents.

1. Insert a table of contents into the proposal.
    a) Navigate to the blank page you inserted earlier after the title page. (This is page 2 in the proposal.) You're going to insert the table of contents on this page.
    b) On the **References** tab, in the **Table of Contents** group, select **Table of Contents** and then **Custom Table of Contents**.
    c) Below **General**, from the **Formats** drop-down list, select **Formal**.
    d) Select **OK**.
    e) Observe the table of contents. All of the text formatted as **Heading 1** is listed in the TOC in bold and all of the text formatted as **Heading 2** is indented under the **Heading 1** item that comes before it in the document.

2. Modify the font for the first-level entries in the table of contents.
    a) On the **References** tab, in the **Table of Contents** group, select **Table of Contents→Custom Table of Contents**.
    b) In the **General** section, from the **Formats** drop-down list, select **From template**.
    c) Select **Modify**.
    d) In the **Style** dialog box, in the **Styles** list box, verify that **TOC 1** is selected and select **Modify**.
    e) In the **Modify Style** dialog box, in the **Formatting** section, from the **Font** drop-down list, select **Times New Roman**.
    f) Deselect **Bold** and select **OK** to close the **Modify Style** dialog box.
    g) Select **OK** to close the **Style** dialog box.
    h) Select **OK** to close the **Table of Contents** dialog box.
    i) In the **Microsoft Word** dialog box, select **Yes** to replace the existing table of contents.
    j) Observe the changes to the table of contents. The modified style is applied to the TOC with Times New Roman font and the main entries are no longer bold.

3. Save the document.

TOPIC D

Insert an Ancillary Table

By including a table of contents and an index, you make looking up content in the document easier, especially when it is printed. Other reference lists are ancillary tables such as a table of figures and a table of authorities. Word makes it easy to generate ancillary tables.

Adding a table of figures to a lengthy document is another way to help the reader find specific information quickly. To avoid readers having to scroll or page through the printed copy, an ancillary table provides a list of references and their corresponding page numbers.

Ancillary Tables

Two common ancillary tables in long reports and other documents are a table of figures and a table of authorities. A table of figures is a list of captions associated with pictures, graphics, and other illustrations with their corresponding page numbers. A table of authorities is a list of references in a legal document with their page numbers. This list can be separated by the type of reference, such as cases, rules, and statutes.

The Table of Figures Dialog Box

You use the **Table of Figures** dialog box to create a table of figures, equations, or tables. Only text to which you have applied the *Caption* style is included in the table.

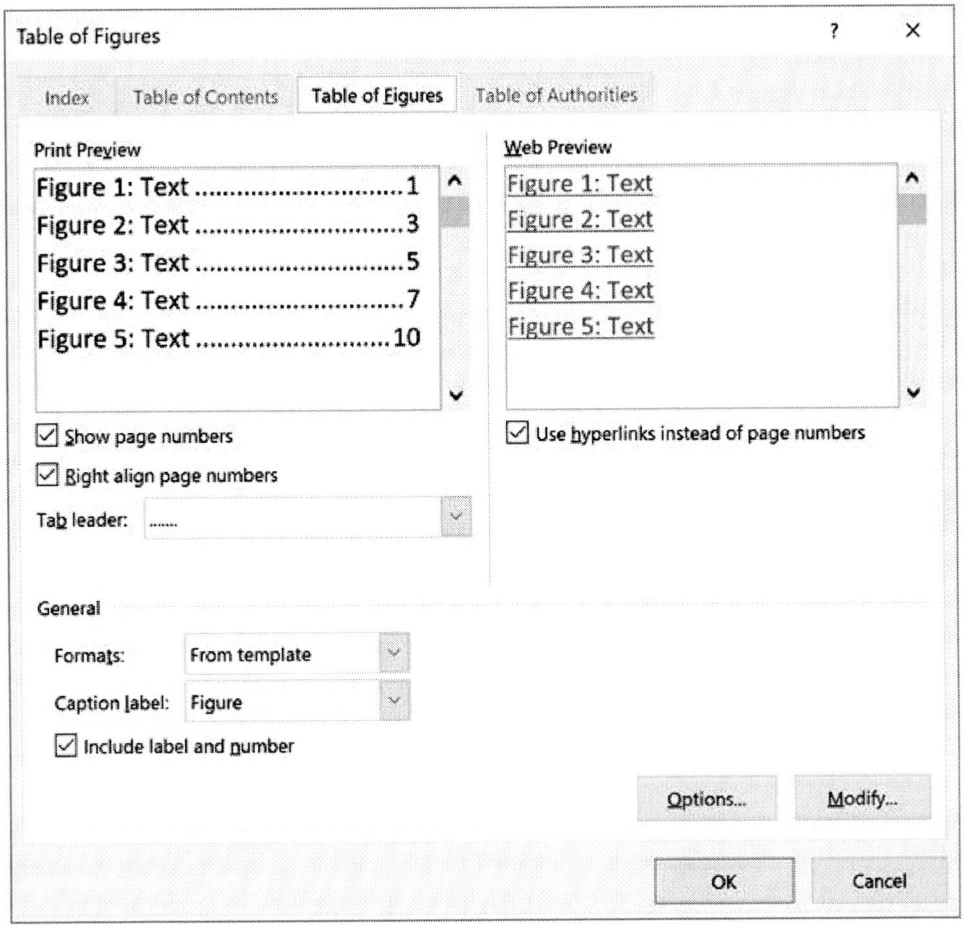

Figure 6-4: The Table of Figures dialog box.

The **Table of Figures** dialog box contains options to insert, format, and modify a table of figures.

Option	Enables You To
Print Preview	Preview the table of figures as it would appear in the printed document.
Web Preview	Preview the table of figures as it would appear on a web page.
Show page numbers	Display the page numbers in the table of figures.
Right align page numbers	Align the page numbers along the right margin of the page.
Tab leader	Set the tab leader format for the page numbers.
Use hyperlinks instead of page numbers	Display the listed page references in the table of figures as hyperlinks, enabling the reader to use the link to navigate to the particular figure.
Formats	Format the table of figures.
Caption label	Select the type of item to include in the table and insert the label into the table entry, such as Table 2: Genres. You can choose whether to build a table of figures, a table of equations, or a table of tables. If you choose **(none)**, no label is included in the table, and you must use the **Table of Figures Options** dialog box to specify which styles to use to create the table.
Include label and number	Display the caption label and number in the table of figures. Uncheck this option to include only the caption text in the table.

Option	Enables You To
Options	Display the **Table of Figures Options** dialog box, which enables you to specify the contents to be included as an entry in the table of figures. The **Style** drop-down list enables you to select the style of text to be included in the table. The **Table entry fields** check box specifies if Word needs to use separate fields for identifying the different tables of figures. You can also specify a table identifier code when your document contains more than one reference table. The table identifier enables Word to identify the tables based on hierarchy.
Modify	Display the **Style** dialog box, which enables you to modify the styles used in the table of figures.

Other Types of Reference Tables

In the **Table of Figures** dialog box, the **Caption label** drop-down list enables you to create other types of reference tables. From the list, select **Table** to create a table of tables. To create a table of equations, from the list, select **Equation**.

 Note: When adding a caption to an object, you have the option to select the caption label as **Figure**, **Table**, or **Equation**. When you want to build a table of figures, table of tables, or table of equations, Word populates the list based on the label you select for the caption.

 Access the Checklist tile on your CHOICE Course screen for reference information and job aids on How to Work with a Table of Figures.

ACTIVITY 6-4
Adding a Table of Figures

Before You Begin
My Building with Heart Proposal.docx is open.

Scenario
The Greene City Council requires that proposals include reference lists of figures and tables as part of the proposal you submit. Using the **Navigation** pane to quickly navigate to the relevant location for the tables, you will generate the table of figures and table of tables.

1. Create a table of figures.
   a) Using the **Navigation** pane, select the heading **TABLE OF FIGURES**.
   b) Position the insertion point in the line below the heading.

   > **Note:** You can use the **Navigation** pane to move to the headings because the Heading1 style was applied to the TABLE OF FIGURES heading in the document.

   c) On the **References** tab, in the **Captions** group, select **Insert Table of Figures**.
   d) If necessary, in the **General** section, from the **Caption label** drop-down list, select **Figure**.
   e) Select **OK**. The table of figures is inserted into the document.

TABLE OF FIGURES
Figure 1 A sample three-bedroom floor plan. 4
Figure 2 Director Chris Baker at work. 7

2. Create a table of tables.
   a) Position the insertion point on the line under the heading **TABLE OF TABLES**.
   b) On the **References** tab, in the **Captions** group, select **Insert Table of Figures**.
   c) In the **General** section, from the **Caption label** drop-down list, select **Table**.
   d) Select **OK** to insert the table.
   e) Save the document.

Table of Authorities

A *table of authorities* is a listing of legal *citations* used in the text, along with their page numbers. Often, a table of authorities appears in legal documents to refer to sources such as cases, rules, treaties, and statutes. Before generating the table of authorities, you must mark all legal citations using the **Mark Citation** button.

The Mark Citation Dialog Box

The **Mark Citation** dialog box contains options to mark the required legal citations before generating a table of authorities. You can use this dialog box to identify cases, statutes, other authorities, rules, treaties, and regulations.

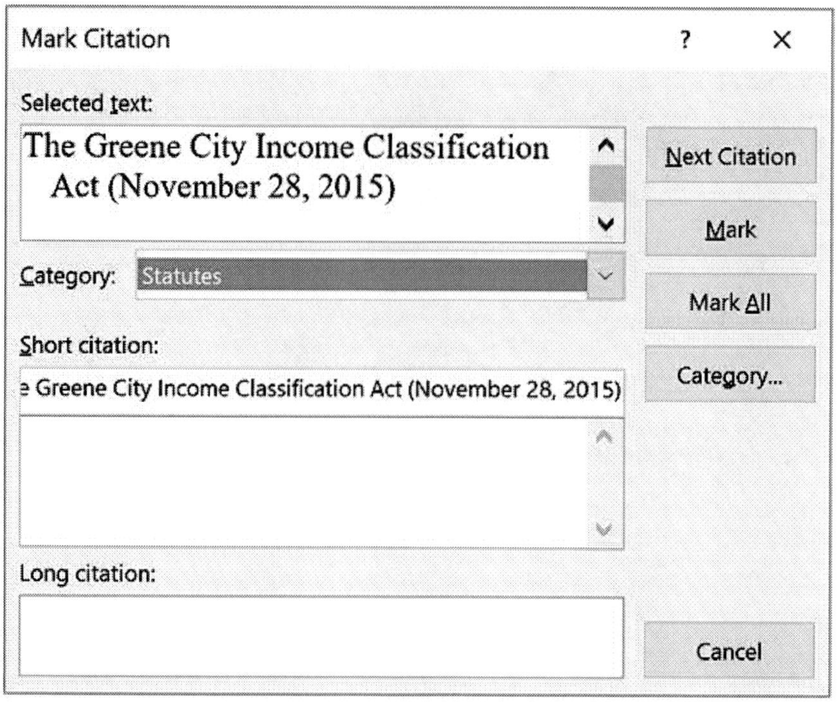

Figure 6–5: The Mark Citation dialog box.

The following table describes the options in the **Mark Citation** dialog box.

Option	Description
Selected text	Displays the selected citation text. This text is editable.
Category	Displays a list of citation categories. You can customize a category by renaming categories 8–16.
Short citation	Enables you to insert the abbreviated citation text that has been applied in the document to following citations of the same source. Word uses this citation text to locate and mark other related citations.
Long citation	Displays the details of a source when you select an existing short citation in the list box under the **Short citation** text box.
Next Citation	Enables you to navigate to the next citation. Word searches for legal terminology such as *re*, *v*, or dates in parentheses.
Mark	Enables you to mark the selected citation as an entry for the table of authorities.
Mark All	Enables you to mark all citations similar to the one entered in the **Selected text** text box.
Category	Displays the **Edit Category** dialog box. This dialog box enables you to replace a selected category of authority with another, and to create a custom category.

Field Code for a Marked Citation

When you mark a citation for a table of authorities entry, Word inserts a field code that resembles { TA \l "Calder v. Jones, 465 U.S. 783 (1984)" \s "Calder, 465 U.S. at 783" \c 1}. The **"\l"** indicates the **Long citation**, the **"\s"** indicates the **Short citation**, and the **"\c"** indicates the

Cases category. To display the field codes for citations, on the **Home** tab, in the **Paragraph** group, select **the Show/Hide ¶** button.

> **Caution:** Mark citations after you have completed editing a document to avoid deleting the field codes in the citations.

The Table of Authorities Dialog Box

The **Table of Authorities** dialog box contains options to insert, format, and modify a table of authorities.

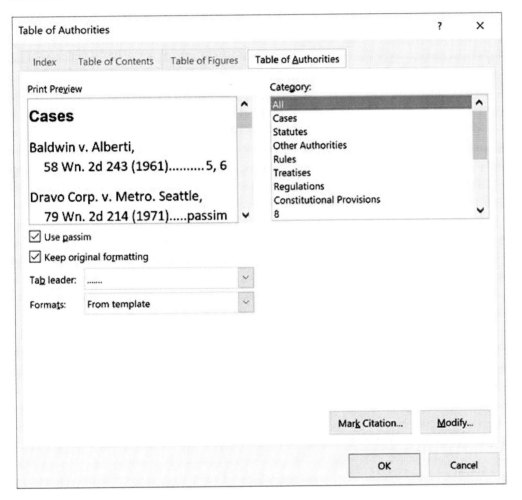

Figure 6–6: The Table of Authorities dialog box.

The following table describes the options available in the **Table of Authorities** dialog box.

Option	Description
Print Preview	Displays a preview of how the table of authorities appears in a document.
Category	Displays a list of categories that you want to include in the table of authorities.
Use passim	Displays the word *passim* next to the citation entry if the same citation has been inserted more than five times.

Option	Description
Keep original formatting	Replicates the format of the marked citations in the table of authorities, which provides for consistent formatting.
Tab leader	Enables you to set the tab leader format for page numbers in the table of authorities.
Formats	Enables you to format the table of authorities.
Mark Citation	Displays the **Mark Citation** dialog box, which you can use to mark additional citations to be included in the table of authorities.
Modify	Displays the **Style** dialog box, which enables you to modify the style of the table of authorities.

Use Passim Option

In the **Table of Authorities** dialog box, the **Use passim** check box is checked by default. *Passim* means "occurs frequently." If there are five or more page references to the same marked legal citation, Word inserts the word "passim" in the table rather than the page numbers when creating the table of authorities.

 Access the Checklist tile on your CHOICE Course screen for reference information and job aids on How to Mark the Text for a Table of Authorities.

 Access the Checklist tile on your CHOICE Course screen for reference information and job aids on How to Add a Table of Authorities.

ACTIVITY 6-5
Adding a Table of Authorities

Before You Begin
My Building with Heart Proposal.docx is open.

Scenario
The proposal contains a few legal citations. For completeness, you include a list of these legal authorities in a table of authorities. First, you will mark the legal citations, and then you will generate the table of authorities.

1. Mark legal citations.
   a) Using the **Navigation** pane, select the heading **Low-Income Applicants**.
   b) In the first sentence after the heading, select the legal citation **The Greene City Income Classification Act (November 28, 2015)**.
   c) On the **References** tab, in the **Table of Authorities** group, select **Mark Citation**.
   d) If necessary, from the **Category** drop-down list, select **Statutes**.
   e) In the **Mark Citation** dialog box, select **Mark**. The dialog box remains open.
   f) Select **Next Citation**. Word automatically selects the next reference to the statute.
   g) Select **Mark**, and then select **Close**.

2. Insert a table of authorities.
   a) In the document, navigate to the heading **TABLE OF AUTHORITIES** and position the insertion point on the line below the heading and before the page break.
   b) On the **References** tab, in the **Table of Authorities** group, select **Insert Table of Authorities**.
   c) In the **Table of Authorities** dialog box, verify that in the **Category** list box, **All** is selected.
   d) From the **Formats** drop-down list, select **Simple**.
   e) Select **OK**.

    Note: Word lists The Greene City Income Classification Act only once in the table of authorities because both references to this act occur on the same page of the document.

   f) Turn off the display of formatting marks.
   g) Close the **Navigation** pane.
   h) Save and close the document.

TOPIC E

Manage Outlines

You have probably heard that the best way to begin a report or complex document is to outline the major topics or sections that you want to include. Setting up the general structure of a complex document ensures that the content is organized in a logical manner. After you have arranged the major sections, you simply need to add content to individual topics to complete the document.

Outline View

An outline is the general organization of a document showing the order of the major topics and subtopics. In Word, **Outline** view displays the headings and indented subheadings in a document when the heading text has been formatted with Word's Heading styles. These headings can be used to reorder the topics in the document and also to navigate to a location within the document. Headings and subheadings can be collapsed or expanded to either hide or show the body text under each heading.

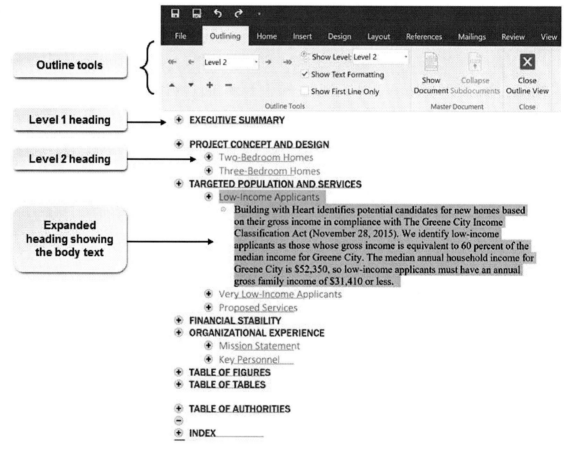

Figure 6-7: Outline view.

> **Note:** In **Outline** view, Word displays only the text formatted with a Heading style. In the **Show Level** drop-down list, if you select **All Levels**, Word displays all headings and body text.

Outline Symbols

In **Outline** view, symbols appear next to content to help visualize the document structure.

Symbol	Indicates
Hidden subheading or body text indicator ✚	The topic contains hidden subtopics or body text.
Hidden subheading indicator Key Personnel	The gray lines displayed under headings indicate that the topic includes body text or subheadings that are not displayed.
No subheading or body text indicator ⊖	The topic does not contain subheadings or body text.
Body text indicator ○	This is body text.

Outline View Tools

On the **Outlining** tab, in the **Outline Tools** group, Word has several tools you use to work with the outline levels.

Tool Name	Description
Promote to Heading 1 ⇇	Promotes the selected item to the highest level in the outline.
Promote ←	Promotes the selected item to the next highest level.
Outline Level Level 1 ▾	Enables you to apply the selected level to an item.
Demote →	Demotes the selected item to the next lower level.
Demote to Body Text ⇉	Demotes the selected item to the lowest level.
Move Up ▲	Moves the selected item up within the outline.
Move Down ▼	Moves the selected item down within the outline.
Expand ✚	Expands the selected item.
Collapse ▬	Collapses the selected item.
Show Level ✛ Show Level: Level 2 ▾	Enables you to choose which levels to display in the outline.

Tool Name	Description
Show Text Formatting 	Displays the outline using the formats applied to the text.
Show First Line Only ☐ Show First Line Only	Shows the first line of each item.
Close Outline View Close Outline View	Closes **Outline** view. Selecting a different view on the **View** tab also closes **Outline** view.

Access the Checklist tile on your CHOICE Course screen for reference information and job aids on **How to Create and Organize an Outline.**

ACTIVITY 6-6
Creating and Organizing an Outline

Data File

Desktop\Building with Heart\Simplifying and Managing Long Documents\Grand Opening Checklist.docx

Scenario

You've been asked to prepare a checklist that HouSalvage store managers can use to train employees and volunteers when Building with Heart opens a new store. To organize your thoughts, you start by creating a simple outline that you will expand on later. You will apply Heading styles in **Outline** view and then reorganize the topics.

1. Open the Grand Opening Checklist.docx document.
   a) In the **Desktop\Building with Heart\Simplifying and Managing Long Documents** folder, open the **Grand Opening Checklist.docx** document.
   b) Save the document as *My Grand Opening Checklist*

2. Create an outline.
   a) Note that the text is formatted with the Normal style.
   b) Position the insertion point in the line containing the text **Grand Opening Checklist**.
   c) Apply the **Heading 1** style to this line of text.
   d) On the **View** tab, in the **Views** group, select **Outline**.
   e) Note that only the heading formatted with the Heading 1 style has a plus sign next to it.

⊕ Grand Opening Checklist
  ◦ **Prepare inventory**
  ◦ **Catalog inventory**
  ◦ **Stock shelves**

3. Promote and demote topics.
   a) Place the insertion point in the phrase **Prepare inventory**.
   b) On the **Outlining** tab, in the **Outline Tools** group, select **Promote**. ⇐
      Note that in the **Outline Level** drop-down list, Word raised this topic to Level 1.
   c) Promote the headings **Create the promotional flyer**, **Plan grand opening events**, **Print signs**, and **Obtain permits** to Level 1.

d) Place the insertion point in the phrase **Catalog inventory** and select **Demote**  to change the text to a lower level.

⊖ Grand Opening Checklist
⊕ Prepare inventory
⊕ Catalog inventory
○ **Stock shelves**

e) Place the insertion point in the phrase **Stock shelves** and select **Promote** to identify this heading as a subtopic below **Prepare inventory**.

f) Promote and demote as necessary the phrases **Identify potential customers** and **Create mailing list** below the **Create the promotional flyer** heading.

4. Add new topics to the outline.

   a) Place the insertion point at the end of the **Plan grand opening events** heading. Press **Enter**.

   b) Note that in the **Outline Level** drop-down list, this new topic is at the same level as the preceding topic. Select **Demote** or press **Tab** to create a subtopic below **Plan grand opening events**.

   c) Type *Contact band director* and press **Enter**.

   d) Type *Order balloons*

5. Change the order of the outline topic headings.

   a) Place the insertion point in the heading **Obtain permits**.

   b) Select **Move Up** ▲ four times to move this topic before **Plan grand opening events**. The topic remains a Level 1 heading. You want to move this topic to the top of the checklist because it's the first step in opening a new store.

   c) To the left of the heading **Obtain permits**, point to the **minus sign**. The cursor changes to a four-headed arrow.

   d) Drag the **Obtain permits** heading so it is the first heading under the heading **Grand Opening Checklist**.

6. Display only certain levels in the outline.

   a) In the **Outline Tools** group, from the **Show Level** drop-down list, select **Level 1**. Word displays only the Level 1 headings.

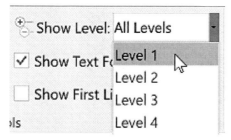

   b) Using the **Show Level** drop-down list, display **All Levels**.

   c) In the **Close** group, select **Close Outline View**.

7. Save the document.

TOPIC F

Create a Master Document

You have worked in a lengthy document using various methods to navigate through the file. An alternative you might choose instead of working in a single long document would be to work with several shorter documents and combine them later. Word can help you handle all of those files through a special type of document that contains links to those subdocuments.

The longer a document becomes, the harder it is to work with, especially when you are collaborating with others. It might be more efficient to break the content into smaller subdocuments. Instead of loading the entire document, you can bring up only the part you want to work on. Then when it's time to print the document, you can use a master document to combine, format, and print all of the subdocuments from one place.

Master Document

A *master document* is a document that contains links to other related documents called *subdocuments*. You can use a master document to organize and maintain a lengthy document by dividing it into smaller, more manageable subdocuments.

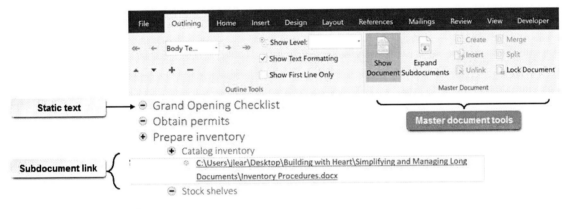

Figure 6-8: A master document.

Benefits of Master Documents

A master document enables you to handle a substantial amount of content by dividing it up into shorter, more manageable subdocuments. If several people need to manipulate the content, they can open only the files on which they need to work. In a master document, you can quickly rearrange subdocuments instead of cutting and pasting large blocks of text or dragging topics around in **Outline** view. Master documents have additional benefits, as well:

- Enabling access to several distinct files from one central location.
- Reducing the file size because the master document doesn't actually contain the subdocument content; rather, it contains links to the subdocuments.
- Providing a convenient means to mark index entries and insert reference tables for content from several documents.
- Allowing for printing of multiple documents without opening each one separately.

Master Document Group

On the **Outlining** tab, the **Master Document** group contains options that help you work with master documents.

> **Caution:** Word displays the options in this group only after you select **Show Document**.

Option	Description
Show Document	Displays the other options in the **Master Document** group.
Collapse Subdocuments/ Expand Subdocuments	Toggles between displaying the full path to the subdocument file and the actual subdocument text.
Create	Creates a new subdocument section in the master document for a heading and generates a new blank document in the same folder as the master document.
Insert	Inserts a link to an existing subdocument file.
Unlink	Deletes the link to the subdocument and copies the subdocument content into the master document.
Merge	Combines the content of two or more subdocuments into one subdocument.
Split	Splits the content of a subdocument into two or more subdocuments.
Lock Document	Locks or unlocks subdocument links so changes made in the master document are not applied to the subdocuments.

> **Note:** You can also lock the subdocuments to prevent other users from modifying the content.

Deleting Subdocument Links from the Master Document

Deleting a subdocument link in the master document removes the connection to the subdocument but does not delete the subdocument file. You cannot undo the deletion of a link.

Unlinking Subdocuments

When you have inserted a subdocument into a master document, it becomes linked to the master and you can then edit it directly from the master document. Word saves all changes you make to a subdocument in the subdocument. To remove the connection between the subdocument and the master document, you must unlink the subdocument. Unlinking a subdocument removes its hyperlink in the master document and copies the subdocument content into the master document.

> **Access the Checklist tile on your CHOICE Course screen for reference information and job aids on How to Create a Master Document.**

ACTIVITY 6-7
Creating a Master Document

Data File

Desktop\Building with Heart\Simplifying and Managing Long Documents\Inventory Procedures.docx

Before You Begin

My Grand Opening Checklist.docx is open.

Scenario

You've started the grand opening checklist and want to insert existing document text under the headings. Some of the documents you intend to include are edited by others and will change. Instead of copying and pasting the text into your document, you create a master document that contains links to the other documents.

---

1. Create a master document.
   a) Save the file **My Grand Opening Checklist** in the current folder as *My Master Checklist.docx*
   b) If paragraph marks and hidden formatting are not displayed, on the **Home** tab, select **Show/Hide ¶**.

    Note: Displaying the paragraph marks and hidden formatting symbols enables you to see the section breaks Word adds when you insert a subdocument.

   c) Switch to **Outline** view.
   d) On the **Outlining** tab, in the **Master Document** group, select **Show Document**.
   e) Place the insertion point after the topic heading **Catalog inventory** and press **Enter**.
   f) In the **Master Document** group, select **Insert**.
   g) Select the file **Inventory Procedures.docx** and select **Open**. Word inserts the content of the document into your master document.
   h) Notice that Word automatically inserted a **Next Page** section break before the content of the subdocument. Delete this section break. You can leave the **Continuous** section break Word also automatically inserted after the subdocument's contents because this section break doesn't affect the flow of the document.
   i) Place the insertion point at the beginning of the paragraph that begins with **Assign items in inventory**. If necessary, from the **Outline Level** drop-down list, select **Body Text** to format the subdocument's contents as body text.
   j) Save the document.
   k) In the **Master Document** group, select **Collapse Subdocuments** to see the links.
   l) On the **View** tab, in the **Views** group, select **Print Layout**. When you collapse the subdocument, the master document shows only the headings and links.

2. Display the subdocument text within the master document.
   a) Switch to **Outline** view.
   b) Select **Expand Subdocuments**. The document now displays the headings and the text in the subdocument.
   c) Switch to **Print Layout** view. You now see the text of the subdocument.

---

d) Save the document.

 Access the Checklist tile on your CHOICE Course screen for reference information and job aids on How to Modify a Master Document.

ACTIVITY 6–8
Modifying a Master Document

Data File

Desktop\Building with Heart\Simplifying and Managing Long Documents\Inventory Procedures.docx

Before You Begin

My Master Checklist.docx is open in **Print Layout** view.

Scenario

You want to make a change in the inserted subdocument below the heading "Catalog inventory." You can open the file from the master document and save changes to the document. After this change, you display the master document with the subdocument text to see how the entire document will look.

---

1. Open a subdocument and edit the file.
   a) Switch to **Outline** view and collapse the subdocuments.
   b) Under the heading **Catalog inventory**, press **Ctrl** and click the link to open the document.
   c) At the end of the first paragraph, add the sentence *Please check for accuracy!*
   d) Save and close the **Inventory Procedures** document.
   e) In the master document, select **Expand Subdocuments** to see that Word displays your change in the master document.

2. Switch to **Print Layout** view. The document shows the headings and the text of the subdocument.

3. Save the file and close Word.

Summary

In this lesson, you learned how to work with long documents and provide the reader with guides to finding information. Reference tables, such as a table of contents and an index, list the location of important information, enabling the reader to quickly jump to that material. Basing your document on an outline organizes the topics from the start as well as allows you to readily reorganize your thoughts. Using a master document to access and combine several separate subdocuments is one way to make working with long documents more manageable.

What types of long documents have you worked on?

Which features do you think a reader finds helpful when reading a lengthy document?

 Note: Check your CHOICE Course screen for opportunities to interact with your classmates, peers, and the larger CHOICE online community about the topics covered in this course or other topics you are interested in. From the Course screen you can also access available resources for a more continuous learning experience.

7 Using Mail Merge to Create Letters, Envelopes, and Labels

Lesson Time: 1 hour

Lesson Objectives

In this lesson, you will use mail merge to create letters, envelopes, and labels. You will:

- Perform a mail merge.

- Merge envelope and label data.

Lesson Introduction

You have seen techniques for standardizing the look and feel of your documents, using Quick Parts and templates to reduce your workload when creating documents, managing the flow of text, and managing long documents. Microsoft® Word includes another useful feature that enables you to automate the creation of documents (such as letters) for a number of recipients. If you have a list of the names, addresses, or other information that needs to go into each separate document, you can use the mail merge feature to customize the documents, which is what you will do in this lesson.

TOPIC A

The Mail Merge Feature

If you have a letter you want to send to every customer of your organization and you want to personalize it with each customer's name and address, you can use the mail merge feature. Rather than manually entering the name and address on each document, you can merge that data into your document, which greatly reduces the time you need to prepare the letters. In this topic, you will perform a simple mail merge in a document.

Mail Merge

A *mail merge* is a process by which a list of data is inserted into a document to create multiple individualized documents. A *main document* contains the static information that will be in all of the documents. It also contains fields into which the variable data will be inserted. The *data source* is a list, a database, a spreadsheet—any type of structured data—that is inserted into the main document during a mail merge. Examples of customized documents you can create include letters, envelopes, labels, and phone and address books.

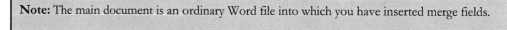 **Note:** The main document is an ordinary Word file into which you have inserted merge fields.

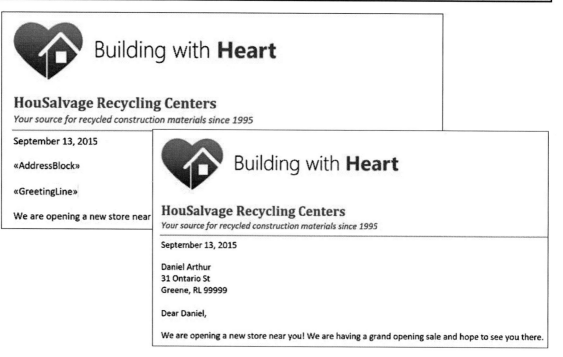

Figure 7–1: Mail merge fields and merge results.

First Name	Last Name	Street	City	State	Zip
Daniel	Arthur	31 Ontario St	Greene	RL	99999
Naomi	Lee	1243 Gaylord Rd	Greene	RL	99999
Gary	Paul	27 Maple Ave	Greene	RL	99999
Ruth	Cross	221 North Jarvis St	Greene	RL	99999
Lori	Patrick	121 Mohawk Tr	Greene	RL	99999
Bob	Thomas	28 Ranch Dr	Greene	RL	99999

Figure 7-2: Data source in a Word table.

Mail Merge Fields

A *merge field* is a placeholder in the merge document into which you want to insert variable data. The merge field provides a link to the variable information in the data source. Word displays the merge field name in your document with double chevrons around the name. The merge field indicates the category of data that Word will insert in your document at the location.

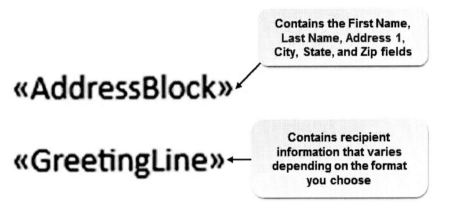

Figure 7-3: Mail merge fields are surrounded by double chevrons.

There are several predefined types of merge fields you can insert in your main document. You can also add other fields using **More Items**, or you can manually insert the other fields in your document.

The merge code is shown by default in the document. If you want to see the data instead, press **Alt +F9** to toggle between the data and the merge code.

Address Block

The **<<Address Block>>** field inserts the name and address from the data source. Word automatically determines which data source fields contain the appropriate name and address data. If your columns are named with something other than the default names, you will need to manually match the data to the fields.

In the example shown in the following figure, the data source uses **Street** rather than **Address 1** as a column heading. Therefore, you need to manually match **Street** and **Address 1**.

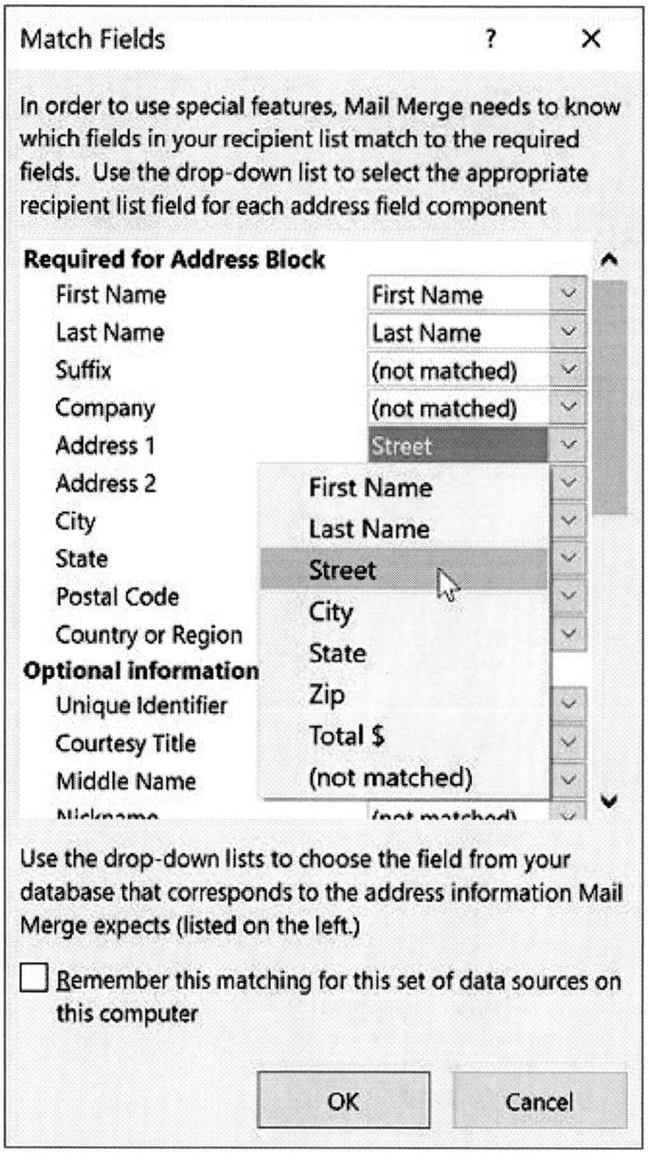

Figure 7-4: If the data source uses different field names than those listed in the Address Block, you need to match mail merge fields to fields in the source document.

Note: Field names with a space in the column header show up in the **Merge Fields** list with an underscore where the space was.

Greeting Line

The **<<Greeting Line>>** field inserts the recipient's name from the data source along with text such as "Dear" or "To" followed by the name and punctuation. By default, it uses the **First Name** and **Last Name** fields from the data source. You can manually select other options.

Insert Greeting Line

Greeting line format:

| Dear | ∨ | Joshua Randall Jr. | ∨ | , | ∨ |

Joshua Randall Jr.
Josh Randall Jr.
Joshua and Cynthia Randall
Josh and Cynthia Randall
Joshua
Josh
Joshua and Cynthia
Josh and Cynthia

Greeting line for in
Dear Sir or Mad

Preview

Here is a preview fr

1

Dear Daniel,

Correct Problems

If items in your greeting line are missing or out of order, use Match Fields to identify the correct address elements from your mailing list.

Match Fields...

OK   Cancel

Figure 7-5: You can configure the Greeting Line field through the Insert Greeting Line dialog box.

More Items

If you have fields that are not part of the address, phone, name, or other fields the **Mail Merge Wizard** knows about, you can use the **More Items** link to add those fields to your document. You can select from **Address Fields** or **Database Fields**. As with the other merge fields, position your cursor in the main document where you want the field to appear, and then insert the merge field. In the following figure, the "$3500" was added through a field in the data sourced named **Total**.

> **Note:** If you select **Address Fields**, all possible fields are listed even if they are not in your data source. The **Database Fields** selection lists only the fields in your data source.

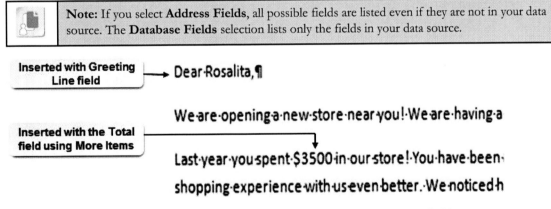

Inserted with Greeting Line field → Dear·Rosalita,¶

We·are·opening·a·new·store·near·you!·We·are·having·a

Inserted with the Total field using More Items → Last·year·you·spent·$3500·in·our·store!·You·have·been·
shopping·experience·with·us·even·better.·We·noticed·h

Figure 7-6: The dollar value was added using the More Items mail merge field.

Electronic Postage

If you have an electronic postage application installed on your computer, you can add the **Electronic Postage** field. If you do not have an electronic postage application installed, you will be prompted to install one.

Rules

There are several rules you can use to programmatically select what data or how data is inserted in the main document from the source data file. For example, you can use *if, then, else* logic to add one block of text if a condition is met or another block of text if the condition is not met. Another rule allows you to skip a record if a condition is not met. The available rules are listed on the **Mailings** tab, in the **Write & Insert Fields** group, from the **Rules** button drop-down list.

The following figure shows an example of using the **If...Then...Else** rule.

Figure 7–7: The mail merge IF rule specifies which field to compare, what to compare it to, and what to insert in the document if it is true or false.

Data Sources

A data source is a document in which information is listed in columns and rows. The columns are categories of information. Each row contains the records for one set of data. The top row of the data source is the header row, which identifies the category of information in that column. The data source can be:

- A database.
- An Outlook® contacts list or address book from another email program.
- Word tables.
- An Excel® worksheet.
- Comma separated value (CSV) or tab separated text files.

In some instances, you'll need to create a list of data for use in a merge document. Two easy ways to create your data source are with a Word table and an Excel worksheet.

Data Guidelines

When you create a data source, no matter which application you use to create it, follow these guidelines:

- The top row of the data must be the field names that categorize the data in each column.
- Each field name in the data source document must be unique.
- Field names should begin with a letter, when possible. If the field name begins with a special character or number, Word adds an alpha character to the beginning of field names in merge fields when you insert them into a merge document.
- Field names must be less than 40 characters; shorter is better.

- If you use spaces in the field name, Word replaces them with underscores in the merge field codes, so try to avoid using spaces.

The Mail Merge Process

There are five main steps in the mail merge process.

Step	Description
1) Create the main document.	This document contains the static text and graphics that will be included in all of the merge documents.
2) Connect the main document and data source.	The data source contains the variable data. It can be an existing document, or you can create a list within the **Mail Merge Wizard**.
3) If desired, specify which records to include.	A copy of the main document is generated for each record in your data source. If you want to create documents for only specific records, you can specify which records to include. For example, only records with a specific ZIP code or only records for people with a failing test score.
4) Insert merge fields into the main document.	Insert the fields from the data source into the main document to link them together. The data source information will replace the placeholder merge fields during the mail merge.
5) Preview and print or email the documents.	You can preview each of the documents prior to printing or emailing the merge documents.

The Mailings Tab

You complete mail merges using the **Mailings** tab. You can use the **Mail Merge Wizard** or manually connect the main document and data source using options on this tab. Until you have started the mail merge process, most of the buttons on the tab are unavailable. When an option is enabled, as on other tabs, the button remains highlighted after you select it. Buttons that you can enable include the **Highlight Merge Fields** and **Preview Results** buttons.

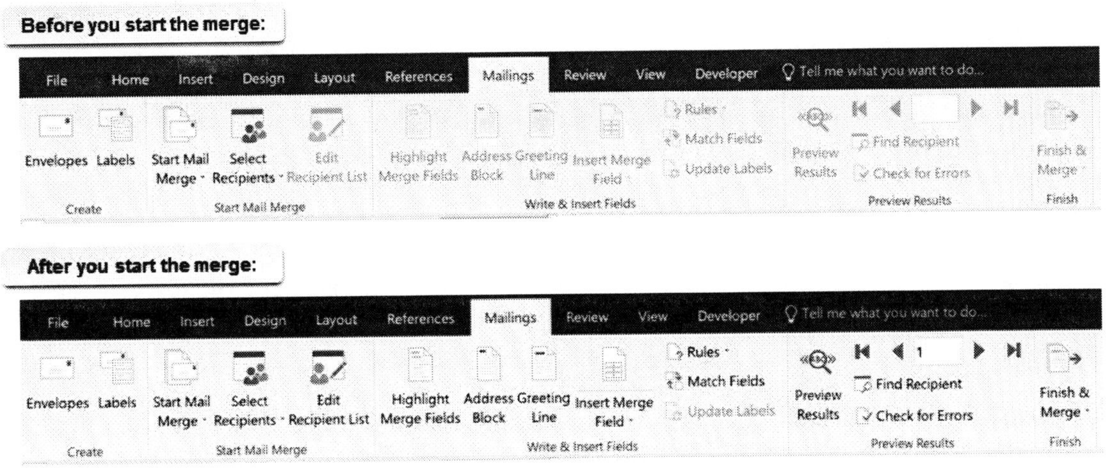

Figure 7–8: The Mailings tab before you start a mail merge (top) and after (bottom).

The Mail Merge Wizard

You can manually insert fields into your main document, or you can use the **Step by Step Mail Merge Wizard**. The wizard is available on the **Mailings** tab, in the **Start Mail Merge** group, from the **Start Mail Merge** drop-down list. There are six steps in the wizard. Each step prompts you for the relevant information to complete the step. The following table describes the steps.

Step	Description
1. Select document type	Choices include letters, envelopes, labels, or directory.
2. Select starting document	Choices include current document, start from a template, or start from existing document.
3. Select recipients	Choices include use an existing list, Outlook contacts, or type a new list.
4. Write your letter	In this step, you insert the merge fields. If necessary, you can also enter the static text in the document.
5. Preview your letters	In this step, you can preview any or all of the merged letters. You can also make changes to the recipient list or exclude a recipient.
6. Complete the merge	In this step, you can print all of the merged documents or edit individual documents.

You don't have to complete the merge all at once. You can save your main merge document. When you open the document later, Word also opens the associated data source. Open the **Mail Merge** task pane to finish the merge.

Merge Dialog Boxes

If you are creating your merge document manually, there are some dialog boxes with which you should become familiar.

Insert Merge Field

You can access the **Insert Merge Field** dialog box in step 4 of the **Mail Merge Wizard** when you select **More Items**, or if you are manually inserting fields, when you select **Insert Merge Field** from the **Write & Insert Fields** group of the **Mailings** tab.

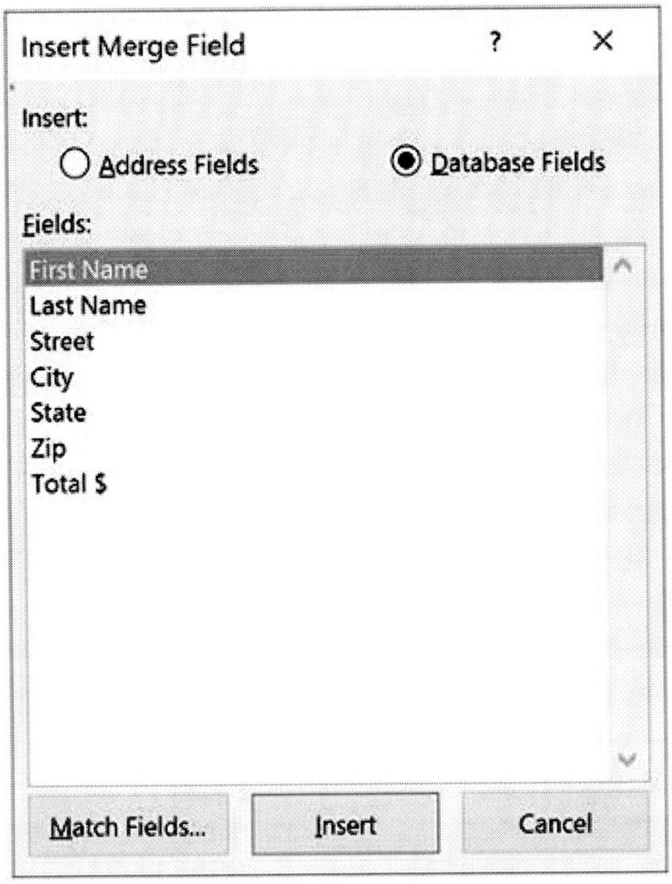

Insert Merge Field

Insert:

○ Address Fields   ● Database Fields

Fields:

First Name
Last Name
Street
City
State
Zip
Total $

Match Fields...   Insert   Cancel

Figure 7-9: You can manually insert fields using the Insert Merge Field dialog box.

Use the **Address Fields** option to select a built-in field that wasn't included in one of the predefined merge blocks you inserted. You also need to use this if the field names in your source data document do not match those in the merge wizard.

Use the **Database Fields** option to insert a field that is not in the predefined list of fields.

Mail Merge Recipients

The **Mail Merge Recipients** dialog box is accessed in step 3 of the **Mail Merge Wizard** when you select **Edit recipient list**. Or, if you are done with the wizard or manually inserting fields, in the **Start Mail Merge** group, select **Edit Recipient List**.

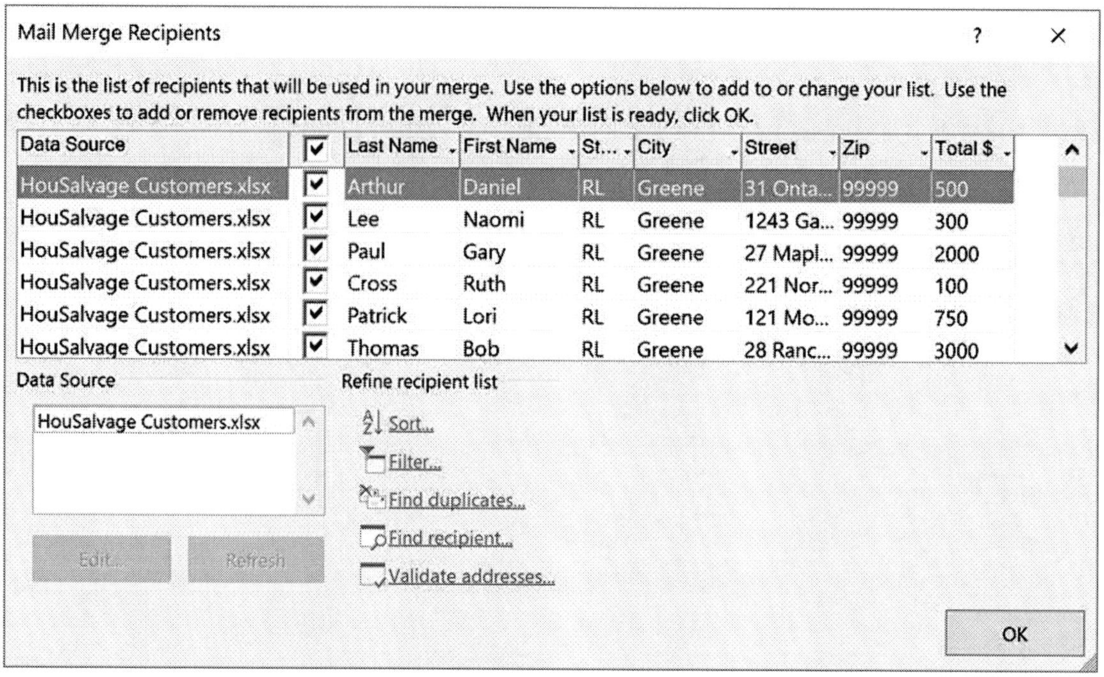

Figure 7-10: Mail Merge Recipients dialog box.

Use this dialog box to add, remove, or edit recipients in the list. You can also sort, filter, find duplicates, find recipients, and validate addresses.

Select **Sort** or **Filter** to display the **Query Options** dialog box. The **Filter Records** tab has options to select the field to filter by, a comparison operation, and what to compare. The **Sort Records** tab has options for which field to sort by and the sort order.

Unlink a Data Source

If you decide that you don't want the document to merge with data from a data source, you can revert the document back to a normal Word document. This is will unlink any fields from the data source. You can leave it as a normal Word document or select another data source to use with the document and set it up again.

Open a Document with a Data Source Attached

When you open a main document that already has a data source attached, Word displays a warning dialog box to let you know that the document will run an SQL command. Select **Yes** to continue opening the document and using the data source.

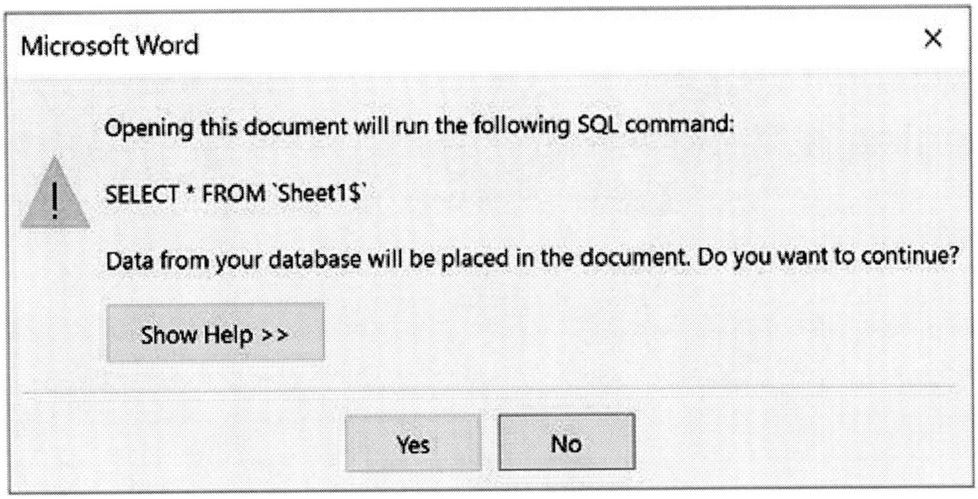

Figure 7–11: This SQL warning message is displayed when you open a source document that has been attached to a data source document.

Access the Checklist tile on your **CHOICE** Course screen for reference information and job aids on **How to Create a Data Source Using Word.**

Access the Checklist tile on your **CHOICE** Course screen for reference information and job aids on **How to Perform a Mail Merge.**

ACTIVITY 7–1
Performing a Mail Merge

Data Files

Desktop\Building with Heart\Using Mail Merge to Create Letters, Envelopes, and Labels \HouSalvage Customers.xlsx

Desktop\Building with Heart\Using Mail Merge to Create Letters, Envelopes, and Labels\New store flyer.docx

Scenario

You created a new store flyer that you want to send to HouSalvage Recycling Center customers. The director of HouSalvage reviewed the letter and asked you to add a greeting line, to add each customer's address, and to personalize it a bit for high-volume customers. You realize that you can accomplish all this by using merge fields. You have an Excel spreadsheet with customer names and addresses you can use for the mail merge.

1. Prepare the **New store flyer.docx** file with merge fields as the main document for the mail merge.
   a) From the **Desktop\Building with Heart\Using Mail Merge to Create Letters, Envelopes, and Labels** folder, open **New store flyer.docx**.
   b) Save the document as *My new store flyer.docx* in the same folder.
   c) On the **Mailings** tab, in the **Start Mail Merge** group, select **Start Mail Merge**.
   d) Select **Step-by-Step Mail Merge Wizard**.
   e) In the **Mail Merge** pane, in the **Select document type** section, verify that **Letters** is selected and then select **Next: Starting document**.
   f) In the **Select starting document** section, verify that **Use the current document** is selected and then select **Next: Select recipients**.

2. Select **Customer data source.xlsx** as the data source for the mail merge.
   a) In the **Mail Merge** pane, in the **Select recipients** section, verify that **Use an existing list** is selected.
   b) Select **Browse**.
   c) Navigate to the **Desktop\Building with Heart\Using Mail Merge to Create Letters, Envelopes, and Labels** folder and select **HouSalvage Customers.xlsx**.
   d) Select **Open**.

e) Verify that **Sheet1$** is selected and that **First row of data contains column headers** is checked.

Select Table   ?   ✕

Name	Description	Modified	Created	Type
Sheet1$		9/13/2015 6:33:07 PM	9/13/2015 6:33:07 PM	TABLE

☑ First r̲ow of data contains column headers   [OK]   [Cancel]

---

f) Select **OK**.

g) Observe the column names. These will become the field names that Word uses to merge data in each record or row from the source document into the main document.

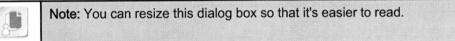 **Note:** You can resize this dialog box so that it's easier to read.

h) In the **Mail Merge Recipients** dialog box, select **OK**.

i) In the **Mail Merge** pane, select **Next: Write your letter**.

3. Insert the **Address block** for the inside address on the letter.

   a) Position the cursor on the blank line above "Dear Customer."

   b) In the **Mail Merge** pane, select **Address block**.

   c) Notice that the name, city, state, and ZIP code are listed in the **Preview**, but the street is not.

   d) Select **Match Fields**.

e) In the **Match Fields** dialog box, select the drop-down to the right of **Address 1** and then select **Street**.

```
Match Fields                              ?      X

In order to use special features, Mail Merge needs to know
which fields in your recipient list match to the required
fields. Use the drop-down list to select the appropriate
recipient list field for each address field component

Required for Address Block                          ^
     First Name          First Name          v
     Last Name           Last Name           v
     Suffix              (not matched)       v
     Company             (not matched)       v
     Address 1           Street              v
     Address 2              First Name       v
     City                   Last Name        v
     State                  Street           v
     Postal Code            City             v
     Country or Region      State            v
Optional information
     Unique Identifier      Zip              v
     Courtesy Title         Total $          v
     Middle Name            (not matched)    v
     Nickname               (not matched)    v

Use the drop-down lists to choose the field from your
database that corresponds to the address information Mail
Merge expects (listed on the left.)

[ ] Remember this matching for this set of data sources on
    this computer

              OK                  Cancel
```

f) Select **OK**. Observe that the address is now correct.
g) Select **OK**.

4. Replace the generic "Dear Customer" with the **Greeting line** merge block.
    a) Select the text "Dear Customer," and then press **Delete** to remove the generic greeting.
    b) In the **Mail Merge** pane, select **Greeting line**.
    c) In the **Insert Greeting Line** dialog box, in the second drop-down list, select **Joshua** and then select **OK**.
    d) Select **Next: Preview your letters**.

5. Preview the main document with data.

a) Select the **Next** button several times to view some of the merged data.

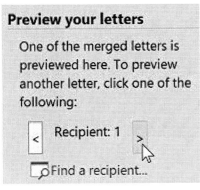

b) Select **Find a recipient**.
c) In the **Find Entry** dialog box, type *Teodoro* and then select **Find Next**.
d) Select **Cancel**.
e) Select **Next: Complete the merge**.

6. Add the **Total_** merge field to the second paragraph with alternate text for high-volume and low-volume customers.

a) Position the cursor at the beginning of the second paragraph in the body of the letter and then type *Last year you spent $*
b) On the **Mailings** tab, in the **Write & Insert Fields** group, select the **Insert Merge Field** drop-down list.
c) Select **Total_**.
d) In the **Write & Insert Fields** group, select the **Rules** drop-down and select **If...Then...Else**.
e) Fill out the **Insert Word Field: IF** with the settings shown in the graphic.

Insert Word Field: IF		? ✕

IF

Field name:	Comparison:	Compare to:
Total_ ⌄	Greater than or equal ⌄	500

Insert this text:

You are a high-volume customer!

Otherwise insert this text:

You are a great customer!

	OK	Cancel

f) Select **OK**.
g) Adjust spacing and punctuation as needed around the inserted fields.

7. Save the merge document for later printing.

a) In the **Mail Merge** pane, select **Edit individual letters**.
b) In the **Merge to New Document** dialog box, verify that **All** is selected and then select **OK**.
c) Scroll through the **Letters1** document to view the merged documents.

    d) Save the **Letters1** document in **Desktop\Building with Heart\Using Mail Merge to Create Letters, Envelopes, and Labels** as *My Merged Letters*

    e) Close **My Merged Letters**.

    f) Save **My new store flyer.docx** in the current folder and then close the file.

TOPIC B

Merge Envelopes and Labels

You have created custom letters using data merged from a list into your main document. You can also create customized envelopes and labels using merge data, which is what you will do in this topic. You will see how you can simply merge the address information and print envelopes or labels as easily as you created merge letters.

Merge Options for Envelopes and Labels

When you create envelopes and labels with merge fields, there are several options you can set. For envelopes, you can set the size, the font, and the position of return and delivery addresses, as well as printing options such as face up or face down. For labels, you can set the label vendor, set the label style number, specify your own dimensions for the label, and give printer information such as continuous-feed printer or a specific printer tray.

Figure 7–12: An envelope with merge fields and merge results.

Create a Single Envelope or Label

If you need to print just a single envelope at any time, you can use this feature. Before you print all of your merged envelopes or labels, you might want to print a single envelope or label to verify that your printer options are correctly configured to print envelopes or labels. The **Mailings** tab includes the option to print a single label or envelope. Instead of merging the data from a data source, you enter the data in the **Envelopes and Labels** dialog box.

Set Up a Return Address

You can use an advanced Word option to configure a return address that Word uses whenever you need to insert your return address on an envelope, label, or letter. To insert the return address wherever you need it, from the **Quick Parts** menu, select **Field**, select **UserAddress**, and then select **OK**.

 Access the Checklist tile on your CHOICE Course screen for reference information and job aids on How to Merge Envelopes and Labels.

ACTIVITY 7-2
Merging Label Data

Data File

Desktop\Building with Heart\Using Mail Merge to Create Letters, Envelopes, and Labels \HouSalvage Customers.xlsx

Scenario

You have created the personalized letters to send out to customers announcing the grand opening of the new store. You need to create address labels to affix to the folded letters so you can mail them to customers. In the supply cabinet, you found Avery 5314 labels.

1. Set the return address to "84 South River Road, Greene City, RL 99999."
   a) Select **File→Options**.
   b) Select the **Advanced** category.
   c) Scroll down to the **General** section.
   d) In the **Mailing address** box, type the following text.

Mailing address:	HouSalvage Recycling Center
	84 South River Road
	Greene City, RL 99999

   e) Select **OK**.

2. Create a merge document for Avery 5314 labels.
   a) Create a new **Blank document**.
   b) To display formatting marks, on the **Home** tab in the **Paragraph** group, select **Show/Hide ¶** to turn on the display of formatting marks.
   c) On the **Mailings** tab, in the **Start Mail Merge** group, select **Start Mail Merge**.
   d) Select **Step-by-Step Mail Merge Wizard**.
   e) Below **Select document type**, select **Labels**, and then select **Next: Starting document**.
   f) Select **Label options**.
   g) From the **Label vendors** drop-down list, select **Avery US Letter**.
   h) From the **Product number** list, select **5314 Mailing Labels**. You can click in the **Product number list** and then type *5314* to jump to the label, or use the scroll bar.
   i) Select **OK**. A blank table with each cell set to the size of an Avery 5314 label is created.

3. Select the recipient data source.
   a) Select **Next: Select recipients**.
   b) With **Use an existing list** selected, select **Browse**.
   c) Browse to **Desktop\Building with Heart\Using Mail Merge to Create Letters, Envelopes, and Labels**, select **HouSalvage Customers.xlsx**, and then select **Open**.
   d) In the **Select Table** dialog box, select **OK**.
   e) In the **Mail Merge Recipients** dialog box, select **OK**.
   f) Select **Next: Arrange your labels**.

4. Insert the **Address block** merge fields and match the field for the **Street** field.
   a) Select **Address block**.
   b) Select **Match Fields**.
   c) From the **Address 1** drop-down list, select **Street**, and then select **OK** twice.
   d) In the **Mail Merge** pane, below **Replicate labels**, select **Update all labels**. Word copies the AddressBlock field to all the labels.

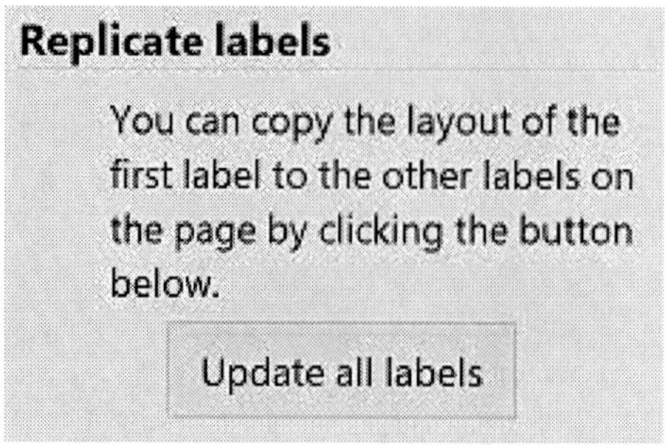

Replicate labels

You can copy the layout of the first label to the other labels on the page by clicking the button below.

Update all labels

   e) Select **Next: Preview your labels**. You now see the table of labels.

5. Save the labels.
   a) In the **Mail Merge** pane, select **Next: Complete the merge**.
   b) In the **Mail Merge** pane, select **Edit individual labels**, and in the **Merge to New Document** dialog box, select **OK**.
   c) Save the label file to the **Desktop\Building with Heart\Using Mail Merge to Create Letters, Envelopes, and Labels** folder as *My Customer Labels*.
   d) Close all open files.

ACTIVITY 7–3
Merging Envelope Data

Data File

Desktop\Building with Heart\Using Mail Merge to Create Letters, Envelopes, and Labels
\HouSalvage Customers.xlsx

Scenario

You are preparing to send a letter to every customer of HouSalvage Recycling Centers. You plan to
send each letter in an envelope and would like to automatically address the envelopes to your
customers.

1. Create an envelope document.
   a) Create a new blank document.
   b) On the **Mailings** tab, in the **Start Mail Merge** group, select **Step-by-Step Mail Merge Wizard**.
   c) Below **Select document type**, select **Envelopes**.
   d) Select **Next: Starting document**.
   e) Below **Change document layout**, select **Envelope options**.

f) In the **Envelope Options** dialog box, observe the default settings.

By default, Word configures envelopes to use the standard business size, **Size 10**, envelope.

g) Select **OK** to close the **Envelope Options** dialog box. Notice that your document now looks like a business envelope.

2. Select the envelope recipients.

a) In the **Mail Merge** pane, select **Next: Select recipients**.

b) Below **Select recipients**, verify that **Use an existing list** is selected and then select **Browse**.

c) Browse to **Desktop\Building with Heart\Using Mail Merge to Create Letters, Envelopes, and Labels**, select **HouSalvage Customers.xlsx**, and then select **Open**.

d) In the **Select Table** dialog box, select **OK**.

e) In the **Mail Merge Recipients** dialog box, select **OK**.

3. Arrange your envelopes.

a) Select **Next: Arrange your envelopes**.

b) Place the insertion point where the addressee information should go. Below **Arrange your envelope**, select **Address block**.

c) Select **Match Fields** and match **Address 1** to the field **Street**. Select **OK** twice. You now see the **<<AddressBlock>>** field in the destination address on the envelope.

4. Preview your envelopes and complete the merge.

a) Select **Next: Preview your envelopes**. Word displays what the envelopes will look like with your data source's information in the **<<AddressBlock>>** field.

b) Select **Next: Complete the merge** to merge the data source and create an envelope for each customer.

c) Select **Edit individual envelopes** and then select **OK** to create a file that contains all the merged envelopes. Word assigns the name **Envelopes** followed by a number to the file.

d) Save the file to **Desktop\Building with Heart\Using Mail Merge to Create Letters, Envelopes, and Labels** as *My Customer Envelopes*

e) Close all open files. If you're prompted to save a file, select **Don't Save**. (You already saved your merged envelopes.)

f) Close Word.

Summary

In this lesson, you created customized labels, envelopes, and letters using the mail merge feature in Word. You also created a data source document in Word for use in a mail merge. This is a useful feature you are likely to use often if you need to send mass mailings in your organization.

How might you use mail merge in your organization?

Will you use the wizard or the manual method for creating mail merge documents? Why?

 Note: Check your CHOICE Course screen for opportunities to interact with your classmates, peers, and the larger CHOICE online community about the topics covered in this course or other topics you are interested in. From the Course screen you can also access available resources for a more continuous learning experience.

Course Follow-Up

Congratulations! You have completed the *Microsoft® Office Word 2016: Part 2* course. You have successfully used a variety of tools to create increasingly complex documents that included section breaks for different page layouts, columns, and text wrapping. You used tools to make your document creation more efficient such as Quick Parts and templates. You also learned how to manage long and complex documents by adding reference tables and creating a master document. In addition, you created customized letters, labels, and envelopes with mail merge.

What's Next?

Microsoft® Office Word 2016: Part 3 is the next course in this series. In this course, you learn use images in documents, add visual interest with custom graphic elements, collaborate on documents, prepare documents for publication, secure documents, create custom forms, and implement macros.

You are encouraged to explore Microsoft Word 2016 further by actively participating in any of the social media forums set up by your instructor or training administrator through the **Social Media** tile on the CHOICE Course screen.

A | Microsoft Office Word 2016 Exam 77-725

Selected Logical Operations courseware addresses Microsoft Office Specialist (MOS) certification skills for Microsoft® Office Word 2016. The following table indicates where Word 2016 skills that are tested on Exam 77-725 are covered in the Logical Operations Word 2016 series of courses.

Objective Domain	Covered In
1 Create and Manage Documents	
1.1 Create a Document	
1.1.1 Create a blank document	Part 1
1.1.2 Create a blank document using a template	Part 1
1.1.3 Open a PDF in Word for editing	Part 1
1.1.4 Insert text from a file or external source	Part 1
1.2 Navigate Through a Document	
1.2.1 Search for text	Part 1
1.2.2 Insert hyperlinks	Part 3
1.2.3 Create bookmarks	Part 3
1.2.4 Move to a specific location or object in a document	Part 2, Topic 2-A; Part 1
1.3 Format a Document	
1.3.1 Modify page setup	Part 1
1.3.2 Apply document themes	Part 2, Topic 2-C
1.3.3 Apply document style sets	Part 2, Topic 2-A
1.3.4 Insert headers and footers	Part 1
1.3.5 Insert page numbers	Part 1
1.3.6 Format page background elements	Part 1
1.4 Customize Options and Views for Documents	
1.4.1 Change document views	Part 1
1.4.2 Customize views by using zoom settings	Part 1
1.4.3 Customize the Quick Access toolbar	Part 1
1.4.4 Split the window	Part 1

Objective Domain	Covered In
1.4.5 Add document properties	Part 3
1.4.6 Show or hide formatting symbols	Part 1
1.5 Print and Save Documents	
1.5.1 Modify print settings	Part 1
1.5.2 Save documents in alternative file formats	Part 1
1.5.3 Print all or part of a document	Part 1
1.5.4 Inspect a document for hidden properties or personal information	Part 3
1.5.5 Inspect a document for accessibility issues	Part 1
1.5.6 Inspect a document for compatibility issues	Part 1
2 Format Text, Paragraphs, and Sections	
2.1 Insert Text and Paragraphs	
2.1.1 Find and replace text	Part 1
2.1.2 Cut, copy and paste text	Part 1
2.1.3 Replace text by using AutoCorrect	Part 1
2.1.4 Insert special characters	Part 1
2.2 Format Text and Paragraphs	
2.2.1 Apply font formatting	Part 1
2.2.2 Apply formatting by using Format Painter	Part 1
2.2.3 Set line and paragraph spacing and indentation	Part 1
2.2.4 Clear formatting	Part 1
2.2.5 Apply a text highlight color to text selections	Part 1
2.2.6 Apply built-in styles to text	Part 1
2.2.7 Change text to WordArt	Part 3
2.3 Order and Group Text and Paragraphs	
2.3.1 Format text in multiple columns	Part 2, Topic 5-C
2.3.2 Insert page, section, or column breaks	Part 2, Topic 5-B
2.3.3 Change page setup options for a section	Part 2, Topic 5-B
3 Create Tables and Lists	
3.1 Create a Table	
3.1.1 Convert text to tables	Part 1
3.1.2 Convert tables to text	Part 1
3.1.3 Create a table by specifying rows and columns	Part 1
3.1.4 Apply table styles	Part 1
3.2 Modify a Table	
3.2.1 Sort table data	Part 2, Topic 1-A
3.2.2 Configure cell margins and spacing	Part 2, Topic 1-B

Objective Domain	Covered In
3.2.3 Merge and split cells	Part 2, Topic 1-B; Part 1
3.2.4 Resize tables, rows, and columns	Part 1
3.2.5 Split tables	Part 1
3.2.6 Configure a repeating row header	Part 1
3.3 Create and Modify a List	
3.3.1 Create a numbered or bulleted list	Part 1
3.3.2 Change bullet characters or number formats for a list level	Part 1
3.3.3 Define a custom bullet character or number format	Part 1
3.3.4 Increase or decrease list levels	Part 1
3.3.5 Restart or continue list numbering	Part 1
3.3.6 Set starting number value	Part 1
4 Create and Manage References	
4.1 Create and Manage Reference Markers	
4.1.1 Insert footnotes and endnotes	Part 3
4.1.2 Modify footnote and endnote properties	Part 3
4.1.3 Create bibliography citation sources	Part 3
4.1.4 Modify bibliography citation sources	Part 3
4.1.5 Insert citations for bibliographies	Part 3
4.1.6 Insert figure and table captions	Part 3
4.1.7 Modify caption properties	Part 3
4.2 Create and Manage Simple References	
4.2.1 Insert a standard table of contents	Part 2, Topic 6-C
4.2.2 Update a table of contents	Part 2, Topic 6-C
4.2.3 Insert a cover page	Part 2, Topic 6-A
5 Insert and Format Graphic Elements	
5.1 Insert Graphic Elements	
5.1.1 Insert shapes	Part 3
5.1.2 Insert pictures	Part 3
5.1.3 Insert a screen shot or screen clipping	Part 3
5.1.4 Insert text boxes	Part 3
5.2 Format Graphic Elements	
5.2.1 Apply artistic effects	Part 3
5.2.2 Apply picture effects	Part 3
5.2.3 Remove picture backgrounds	Part 3
5.2.4 Format objects	Part 3
5.2.5 Apply a picture style	Part 3

Objective Domain	Covered In
5.2.6 Wrap text around objects	Part 3
5.2.7 Position objects	Part 1
5.2.8 Add alternative text to objects for accessibility	Part 1
5.3 Insert and Format SmartArt Graphics	
5.3.1 Create a SmartArt graphic	Part 3
5.3.2 Format a SmartArt graphic	Part 3
5.3.3 Modify SmartArt graphic content	Part 3

B | Microsoft Office Word 2016 Expert Exam 77-726

Selected Logical Operations courseware addresses Microsoft Office Specialist (MOS) certification skills for Microsoft® Office Word 2016. The following table indicates where Word 2016 skills that are tested on Exam 77-726 are covered in the Logical Operations Word 2016 series of courses.

Objective Domain	Covered In
1 Manage Document Options and Settings	
1.1 Manage Documents and Templates	
1.1.1 Modify existing templates	Part 2, Topic 4-B
1.1.2 Copy custom styles, macros, and building blocks to other documents or templates	Part 2, Topics 3-A, 3-B, 4-C
1.1.3 Manage document versions	Part 3
1.1.4 Compare and combine multiple documents	Part 3
1.1.5 Link to external document content	Part 2, Topics 1-E, 5-D
1.1.6 Enable macros in a document	Part 3
1.1.7 Display hidden ribbon tabs	Part 1; Part 3
1.1.8 Change the application default font	Part 2, Topic 2-A
1.2 Prepare Documents for Review	
1.2.1 Restrict editing	Part 3
1.2.2 Mark a document as final	Part 3
1.2.3 Protect a document with a password	Part 3
1.3 Manage Document Changes	
1.3.1 Track changes	Part 3
1.3.2 Manage tracked changes	Part 3
1.3.3 Lock or unlock tracking	Part 3
1.3.4 Add comments	Part 3
1.3.5 Manage comments	Part 3
2 Design Advanced Documents	

Objective Domain	Covered In
2.1 Perform Advanced Editing and Formatting	
2.1.1 Find and replace text by using wildcards and special characters	Part 1
2.1.2 Find and replace formatting and styles	Part 1
2.1.3 Set advanced page setup layout options	Part 1
2.1.4 Link text boxes	Part 2, Topic 5-D
2.1.5 Set paragraph pagination options	Part 2, Topic 5-A
2.1.6 Resolve style conflicts by using Paste Options	Part 1
2.2 Create Styles	
2.2.1 Create paragraph and character styles	Part 2, Topic 2-A; Part 1
2.2.2 Modify existing styles	Part 2, Topic 2-A
3 Create Advanced References	
3.1 Create and Manage Indexes	
3.1.1 Mark index entries	Part 2, Topics 6-B, 6-F
3.1.2 Create indexes	Part 2, Topic 6-B
3.1.3 Update indexes	Part 2, Topic 6-B
3.2 Create and Manage References	Part 1; Part 3
3.2.1 Customize a table of contents	Part 2, Topic 6-C; Part 1
3.2.2 Insert and modify captions	Part 1; Part 3
3.2.3 Create and modify a table of figures	Part 2, Topic 6-D
3.3 Manage Forms, Fields, and Mail Merge Operations	
3.3.1 Add custom fields	Part 3
3.3.2 Modify field properties	Part 3
3.3.3 Perform mail merges	Part 1; Part 3
3.3.4 Manage recipient lists	Part 2, Topic 7-A
3.3.5 Insert merged fields	Part 2, Topic 7-A
3.3.6 Preview merge results	Part 2, Topic 7-A
4 Create Custom Word Elements	
4.1 Create and Modify Building Blocks, Macros, and Controls	
4.1.1 Create QuickParts	Part 2, Topics 3-A, 3-B
4.1.2 Manage building blocks	Part 2, Topic 3-B
4.1.3 Create and modify simple macros	Part 3
4.1.4 Insert and configure content controls	Part 3
4.2 Create Custom Style Sets and Templates	
4.2.1 Create custom color sets	Part 2, Topic 2-C
4.2.2 Create custom font sets	Part 2, Topic 2-C

Objective Domain	Covered In
4.2.3 Create custom themes	Part 2, Topic 3-C
4.2.4 Create custom style sets	Part 2, Topic 2-A
4.3 Prepare a document for Internationalization and Accessibility	
4.3.1 Configure language options in documents	Part 2 Topics 2-A, 6-B; Part 1
4.3.2 Add alt-text to document elements	Part 1
4.3.3 Manage multiple options for +Body and +Heading fonts	Part 2, Topic 2-A
4.3.4 Utilize global content standards	Part 1

C | Microsoft Word 2016 Common Keyboard Shortcuts

The following table lists common keyboard shortcuts you can use in Word 2016.

Function	Shortcut
Open a document	Ctrl+O
Create a new document	Ctrl+N
Save a document	Ctrl+S
Undo an action	Ctrl+Z
Redo or repeat an action	Ctrl+Y
Bold the selected text	Ctrl+B
Italicize the selected text	Ctrl+I
Underline the selected text	Ctrl+U
Copy the selected text	Ctrl+C
Paste the copied text	Ctrl+V
Open the **Navigation** pane to search a document	Ctrl+F
Switch to print preview	Alt+Ctrl+I
Print a document	Ctrl+P
Insert a review comment	Alt+Ctrl+M
Go to the beginning of a document	Home
Go to the end of a document	End
Insert a hyperlink	Ctrl+K
Insert a line break	Shift+Enter
Insert a page break	Ctrl+Enter
Insert a column break	Ctrl+Shift+Enter
Change the case of the selected letters	Shift+F3
Capitalize all selected letters	Ctrl+Shift+A
Preview a mail merge	Alt+Shift+K

Function	Shortcut
Merge a document	**Alt+Shift+N**

Mastery Builders

Mastery Builders are provided for certain lessons as additional learning resources for this course. Mastery Builders are developed for selected lessons within a course in cases when they seem most instructionally useful as well as technically feasible. In general, Mastery Builders are supplemental, optional unguided practice and may or may not be performed as part of the classroom activities. Your instructor will consider setup requirements, classroom timing, and instructional needs to determine which Mastery Builders are appropriate for you to perform, and at what point during the class. If you do not perform the Mastery Builders in class, your instructor can tell you if you can perform them independently as self-study, and if there are any special setup requirements.

Mastery Builder 1-1
Organizing Content Using Tables and Charts

Activity Time: 20 minutes

Data File

Desktop\Building with Heart\Organizing Content Using Tables and Charts\Current Projects.docx

Scenario

You have been given a list of Building with Heart's current construction projects that was created by a volunteer. The volunteer entered the projects in no particular order. In preparation for the monthly staff meeting, you need to sort the table containing the projects in order by project manager and then project number. In addition, you want to provide a total cost for each of the projects. Finally, you want to add a chart that compares the total project costs assigned to each project manager.

1. In **Desktop\Building with Heart\Organizing Content Using Tables and Charts**, open **Current Projects.docx** and save the file in the current folder as *My Current Projects*

2. Add the appropriate formula in the **Total Cost** column to calculate the total cost of each project. Format the results to show two decimal places.

    Note: Hint: You can copy the first formula and paste it in the remaining column cells, then press **F9** to update the results.

3. Sort the table by **Project Manager** and then by **Project Number**.

4. Merge the appropriate cells in the **Project Manager** column and delete the duplicates.

5. Sort the second table in order by **Project Manager**.

6. In the second table, for each project manager, calculate the total cost of their projects.

7. Create a clustered column chart that shows the total cost of projects assigned to each project manager.

8. Resize the chart so that it will fit on the first page.

9. Save the file.

10. Compare your results to the solution provided.

Mastery Builder 2-1
Customizing Formats Using Styles and Themes

Activity Time: 10 minutes

Data File

Desktop\Building with Heart\Customizing Formats Using Styles and Themes\Specials.docx

Scenario

Every month, you have to create a sales flyer with the HouSalvage Recycling Center monthly specials. You have been creating it from scratch or copying and changing an existing file with the new data, but sometimes you miss some of the items and they are left in the current flyer. Now that you know how to use styles and themes, you realize how much time you could save and the potential to reduce the number of errors you might make when you create the new flyers. Every flyer needs the store name in the correct colors and fonts, a bulleted list of items included in the sale, a table of sale items, and a special story about one of the employees who helped a customer. You have the existing flyer from last month and will use that to create styles to apply to this month's flyer.

1. From the **Desktop\Building with Heart\Customizing Formats Using Styles and Themes** folder, open **Specials.docx**.

2. Save the document as *My Specials.docx*

3. Create a new paragraph style named **HouSalvage** based on the HouSalvage Recycling Center paragraph at the top of the document.

4. Create a new paragraph style named **Tagline** based on the second line.

5. Create a new text style named **FlyerHeading** based on the heading "Store Locations." Apply this style to the other headings in the flyer.

6. Create a new table style named **Locations** based on the table containing the store locations and hours.

7. Create a new list style named **SaleItems** based on the list with the shopping cart bullets.

8. Create a new text style named **FlyerText** based on the text under the heading "Employee of the Month."

9. Create a new document that uses the styles you just created.

10. Save and close the file.

Mastery Builder 3-1
Inserting Content Using Quick Parts

Activity Time: 20 minutes

Data File

Desktop\Building with Heart\Inserting Content Using Quick Parts \BuildingBlocks.docx

Scenario

You are putting together the newsletter for the HouSalvage Recycling Center. You have to create this document each month. You use some of the components for the newsletter in other documents throughout the Building with Hearts organization. To keep documents looking consistent, you decide to create Quick Part building blocks.

1. From the **Desktop\Building with Heart\Inserting Content Using Quick Parts** folder, open **BuildingBlocks.docx**.

2. Create a Quick Part that consists of the Building with Heart logo, HouSalvage Recycling Centers, and the tagline.

3. Create a Quick Part of the list of jobs for which HouSalvage is hiring.

4. On page 2, create a Quick Part of the header (HouSalvage Recycling Centers News and today's date).

5. Create a Quick Part of the footer.

6. Create a new document.

7. Use the Quick Parts you just created to add content to the document.

8. Add a date field near the top of the document.

9. Save the file in the current folder as *My Quick Parts Mastery Builder*

Mastery Builder 4–1
Using Templates to Automate Document Formatting

Activity Time: 15 minutes

Data File

Desktop\Building with Heart\Using Templates to Automate Document Formatting\HouSalvage Spring Newsletter.docx

Scenario

In the past, you have created the quarterly newsletters for HouSalvage Recycling Centers from scratch. Now that you know about document templates, you want to create a template you can use in the future for newsletters.

---

1. From the **Desktop\Building with Heart\Using Templates to Automate Document Formatting** folder, open **HouSalvage Spring Newsletter.docx**.

2. In place of the **Volume 1, Issue 1** line, add a MacroButton field that prompts you for the volume and issue numbers.

3. Delete all the content in the newsletter except for the **Employee of the Quarter** section. You plan to include this section in every HouSalvage newsletter.

4. In the **Employee of the Quarter** section, delete the content and add a MacroButton field that prompts you to add information about the employee.

5. Delete the photo from the box on the right side of the **Employee of the Quarter** section. Resize the box as necessary and add the text *Insert employee photo here* to the box.

6. Delete the quote in the second text box and replace it with *Insert employee quote here*

7. Save this document as a template and close it.

8. Create a new document using the template you just created.

9. Save the document in the current folder as *My HouSalvage Newsletter* and then close the document.

Mastery Builder 5-1
Controlling the Flow of a Document

Activity Time: 15 minutes

Data Files

- Desktop\Building with Heart\Controlling the Flow of a Document\Building with Heart Newsletter.docx
- Desktop\Building with Heart\Controlling the Flow of a Document\HouSalvage Recycling Centers.docx

Scenario

You are creating a newsletter for Building with Heart. You have the basic content in the newsletter but would like to make it more attractive and easier to read. You have decided to use columns for some of the content to improve the newsletter's appearance. In addition, you want to add some of the information about HouSalvage Recycling Centers on the first page in a text box and have the rest of the information appear in a text box at the end of the newsletter.

1. From the **Desktop\Building with Heart\Controlling the Flow of a Document** folder, open **Building with Heart Newsletter.docx**.

2. Format the first paragraph, the "Our Mission" section, and the "Spring Update" section to use a column layout of your own choosing.

3. Draw a text box in the bottom-right corner of the first page. Select **Layout Options** and then below **With Text Wrapping**, select **Square** so that Word wraps the content around the text box instead of the content being hidden behind the text box.

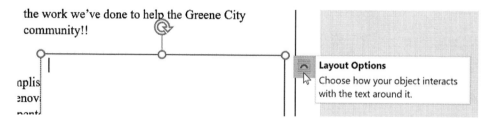

4. Add a second text box at the end of the newsletter and configure it to use square text wrapping. Link these two text boxes together.

5. Insert the text of the **HouSalvage Recycling Centers.docx** document into the text boxes. Adjust the text boxes so that the entire contents of the document appear.

6. Add text boxes above or below the linked text boxes to indicate where the reader can find the rest of the story.

7. Adjust the other stories so that the content fits onto single pages. Use paragraph flow control, page and section breaks, and columns as you see fit to make this possible.

8. Save the file in the current folder as *My Building with Heart Newsletter*

Mastery Builder 6–1
Simplifying and Managing Long Documents

Activity Time: 15 minutes

Data File

Desktop\Building with Heart\Simplifying and Managing Long Documents\History.docx

Scenario

You are starting to work on a document about the history of HouSalvage Recycling Centers. So far you have some headings and a little bit of text. To make it easier to create a table of contents, you want to prepare the headings so that Word automatically includes them in that reference table. You also want to try out some cover page designs.

1. Open the file **History.docx**.

2. Format the existing headings using at least two different Heading styles.

3. Generate a table of contents using the **Formal** style.

4. Change the table of contents format to another style.

5. Insert a cover page at the beginning of the document.

6. Enter text for the document **Title** and **Subtitle** placeholders. Delete any other placeholders.

7. Select a different cover page design and apply it to the document.

8. Save the file as *My History.docx* and close the file.

Mastery Builder 7-1

Using Mail Merge to Create Letters, Envelopes, and Labels

Activity Time: 20 minutes

Data File

Desktop\Building with Heart\Using Mail Merge to Create Letters, Envelopes, and Labels\Vendor Letter.docx

Scenario

You are preparing letters to go out to vendors. You want to personalize the letters to include the type of merchandise you purchase from the vendor, along with the vendor contact's name and address. You plan to mail these out in envelopes so you want to also merge the vendor addresses into envelopes for printing.

---

1. Create a data source document named **Vendors** with five vendor names, addresses, and one product for each vendor. (You can use Word or Excel to create the data source document, or you can type the list as part of the merge process—your choice.)

2. From the **Desktop\Building with Heart\Using Mail Merge to Create Letters, Envelopes, and Labels** folder, open **Vendor Letter.docx**.

3. In the **Vendor Letter** file, select your data source document to merge.

4. In the **Vendor Letter** file, insert the address block for the vendor to replace the placeholder text for the inside address.

5. Insert the product field to replace the product placeholder.

6. Review the merged documents.

7. Save the merged documents to a file in the current folder for printing at a later time.

8. Create envelopes with the vendors' addresses.

9. Save the merged envelope documents in the current folder for printing at a later time.

Glossary

arguments
Entities within the parentheses following a function name in a formula.

building block
Content that has been formatted and stored for use in any Word document.

caption
A phrase that describes an object such as a picture, graphic, equation, or table.

cell alignment
Enables you to position the cell contents in one of nine positions.

cell merging
Combines multiple adjacent cells into a single cell that is the size and shape of the original cells.

cell splitting
Divides one or more cells into multiple adjacent cells.

character spacing
Formatting that allows you to control the size of characters and the space between characters.

character style
Defines the formatting to apply to text.

chart
A graphical interpretation of data.

citation
A reference to any legal source of content.

concordance file
A document used to automatically mark index entries in another document.

cover page
An attractive first page containing information such as the title, author's name, and date.

custom style
User-defined formatting characteristics for characters or paragraphs.

data source
A list, database, or spreadsheet that is inserted into the main document during a mail merge.

document theme
A THMX file that contains a set of theme colors, fonts, and effects such as lines and fill effects.

equation
A document element for adding complex mathematical symbols to your document.

field
A placeholder that displays variable data.

field codes
Programming that processes the command identified in the field code and displays the result as a field value.

formula
A type of field code used to perform mathematical calculations on data in a table.

function
The action that will be performed on the values in a formula.

kerning
Adjust spacing between specific letter pairs so that the spacing appears even.

linked style
A style that contains both character and paragraph formatting.

mail merge
A process by which a list of data is inserted into a document to create multiple individualized documents.

main document
Contains the static information used for merge documents and the fields into which the variable data will be inserted.

mask
Specifies the format numbers will take, such as formatting with dollar signs or percent signs and specifying the number of decimal places to use.

master document
A document that contains links to other related documents called subdocuments.

merge field
A placeholder in the merge document that variable data is inserted into.

orphans
Single lines at the bottom of a page separated from the rest of the paragraph of which they are a part.

paragraph style
Formats the paragraph appearance as well as all of the formatting included in character styles.

section break
Divides a document into sections where a different page layout can be configured for each section of the document.

sorting
Table data is arranged in ascending or descending alphabetical or numerical order.

style
A set of formatting characteristics.

subdocument
A document linked to a master document.

table of authorities
A listing of legal citations used in the text.

template
A special type of Word document containing the desired formatting that you can use as the starting point for creating new Word documents.

text box
A Word object that enables you to place text anywhere in your document.

text direction
An option that enables you to position the text horizontally or vertically in a table cell.

text wrapping
An option used to arrange images and text in a document.

widows
Single lines at the top of a page separated from the rest of the paragraph of which they are a part.

Index